The Children's Media Yearbook is a publication of The Children's Media Foundation

Director, Greg Childs
Administrator, Jacqui Wells

The Children's Media Foundation
15 Briarbank Rd
London
W13 0HH

info@thechildrensmediafoundation.org

First published 2020

© Diana Hinshelwood for editorial material and selection
© Individual authors and contributors for their contributions

All rights reserved. No part of this publication may be reproduced, stored in a retrieval system, or transmitted, in any form or by any means, without the prior permission in writing of The Children's Media Foundation, or as expressly permitted by law, or under terms agreed with the appropriate reprographics rights organisation. You must not circulate this book in any other binding or cover.

ISBN 978-1-9161353-3-8

Book design by Camilla Umar
Cover image by Cory Woodward on Unsplash

CHILDREN'S MEDIA YEARBOOK 2020

EDITORIAL

2020 VISION
How World Events in 2020 Changed Children's Media
Diana Hinshelwood — 4

THE IMPACT OF UNPRECEDENTED TIMES
Greg Childs — 6

THE ISSUES AHEAD
Anna Home OBE — 9

STATE OF PLAY

CREATIVITY IS MAGIC, AND MAGIC IS FOR EVERYONE
Cressida Cowell — 14

PLAY AND THE ART OF PLAYFUL COMMUNICATION
Ash Perrin — 17

WHAT'S IN THE BRIEFCASE?
David Kleeman — 21

CHILDREN ARE AWESOME
Hazel Kenyon — 25

THE BUNNY FROM BROOKLYN
BUGS BUNNY'S 80TH Birthday — 29

FRIENDS

KIDS MEDIA WORLDS RIGHT NOW
Maxine Fox — 33

THE RISE OF 'THE VLOGGER NEXT DOOR'
Jessica Rees — 36

BIG STEPS FOR LITTLE RADIO
Chris Jarvis — 40

MODERN FAMILY

BLACK LIVES MATTER:
What Does It Mean for the Children's Media Industry?
Zoë Daniel — 43

IS THIS OK?
Lucy Edwards — 47

MISSION EMPLOYABLE:
Presenting Popular Shows in BSL
Cecilia Weiss — 50

REMEMBER, REMEMBER: THE TWENTIETH OF NOVEMBER:
United Nations Convention on the Rights of the Child
Jayne Kirkham — 53

STRANGER THINGS

UNDERSTANDING KIDS' SVOD HABITS
Helen Lockett and Ryan Lewis — 58

6 EXPERT TIPS FOR PRODUCING INTERACTIVE TV SHOWS
Kate Dimbleby — 62

LIVE THEATRE FOR KIDS
How Digital Can Make A Difference
Nathan Guy — 66

CREATING CONTENT FOR KIDS AND TEENS WITH 2020 VISION 68
Pete Maginn

A PURPOSEFUL FUTURE 72
Bruna Capozzoli

THE OFFICE

RADICAL THINKING: 76
Can A New Public Service Broadcast Concept Reshape The Children's Media Landscape?
Colin Ward

BBC BITESIZE DAILY AND LOCKDOWN 78
Helen Foulkes

TIDINGS OF CONTENT AND JOY 81
The Progress of the Young Audiences Content Fund
Jackie Edwards

THE GENERATION GAME

THE GENERATION GAME 85
Can The BBC Win Over Today's Young Audience
Michael Wilson and Neil Fowler

OK BOOMERS! HERE ARE OUR CHALLENGES AND OPPORTUNITIES 85
Victoria McCollum

GEN Z - PUBLIC SERVICE TV'S LOST GENERATION 90
Claire Hungate

A TIK-TOKING CLOCK HEADING TOWARDS REGENERATION – OR NOT?: 95
Colin Mann

THE SESAME STREET EFFECT 99
What it means for UK broadcasters and their black and Asian audiences
Marcus Ryder

THE EDITORS 104

AFTERLIFE

MICHAEL ANGELIS 106
Sharon Miller

DEREK FOWLDS 108
Diana Hinshelwood

LORD GORDON OF STRATHBLANE 110
Jayne Kirkham

YOU DID IT!

CONTRIBUTORS 111

CMF YEARBOOK EDITORIAL 2020 VISION:

How World Events in 2020 Changed Children's Media.

DIANA HINSHELWOOD

Editor, Children's Media Yearbook 2020

2020 Vision. If only we'd had that at the beginning of the year 2020. Would we have done anything different? In January, rumours of a deadly virus were just that – rumours. There was a sense that it was happening far away and wouldn't affect us. But we were wrong, and by March the world as we knew it had changed – perhaps forever. The impact was instant and powerful.

Digital changes have been under way for some time in the media industry, but world events in 2020 have accelerated those changes. Of course, the industry was affected, halting new productions and causing unemployment in cast and crew. For the Children's Media Foundation, it meant no physical Children's Media Conference for 2020, the annual industry get-together in Sheffield.

However, not to be beaten by a mere virus, the Children's Media Conference team took advantage of digital's ability to bring people together on-line. It was a massive effort by the CMC team and the many industry professionals who made it happen, and we owe them a huge debt of gratitude.

As there was no simple physical method of distributing the Yearbook to industry professionals as in previous years, we decided to put the Children's Media Yearbook 2020 on-line too. We have opinions, research, serious issues and even some good news, so there's no need to feel you've missed out on any of the discussions that have occupied us in this strange year.

Viewing habits were changed as a result of being forced inside. Children and young people suffered from the restrictions as school, meeting friends and fresh air disappeared. An appetite for content that portrayed how lockdown felt, as well as a desire for self-produced content to reflect young lockdown lives became apparent. The way the young audience use media has also been changing for some time but the lack of physical contact with friends saw an increase in social media apps and platforms that enabled the audience to stay in touch with each other. Research highlights some surprising and not so surprising Covid viewing trends.

Some sections of the media benefitted from lockdown, such as Radio. Others were completely devastated, such as Live Theatre. However, amongst the despair of Theatreland, digital was able to provide some respite, but is it enough?

Covid 19 has not been the only world event to change the shape of content. Events like Black Lives Matter and issues around Inclusivity such as Trans Rights and Disability Access have had a profound impact on the young audience, who care deeply about them and are more accepting of difference than previous generations. In this Yearbook, we explore these huge themes and their effect on Children's Media content – largely driven by changemakers and young film makers themselves.

And of course, we can't talk about the effect of Covid 19 and digital without considering the future of Public Service Broadcasting – and by extension the future of the BBC. The extraordinary events caused by Covid 19 throw a light on the importance of PSB, but also cast a shadow on how it should be delivered. *BBC Bitesize Daily* was one of the Corporation's successes this year, but again the question, is it enough to save it? It's an important and on-going discussion which The Children's Media Foundation plan to continue and we hope you join the discussion.

The Children's Media Foundation would not be able to continue in its work in ensuring UK children have access to the best possible media, on all platforms, at all ages without our patrons and donors. We rely on their donations to fund that work and we're very grateful for their support. Covid 19 and has not gone away, and the changes its wrought provide us with much work still to do. We need to be ahead of the game to keep up with the fast pace of world events and we would welcome your support as a donor or patron www.thechildrensmediafoundation.org/support.

Thank you to all the contributors who wrote and re-wrote articles, and without whom there'd be no Yearbook. The good nature and willingness that greeted a request for contributions at short notice and a tight deadline was amazing. Thank you also to our designer Camilla Umar, who guided me through the process and made it feel less daunting. It is a testament to the tenacity and creativity of the media industry when faced with a challenge.

Diana

CHILDREN'S MEDIA FOUNDATION ANNUAL REPORT THE IMPACT OF UNPRECEDENTED TIMES

GREG CHILDS
Director, The Children's Media Foundation

As we emerge from lockdown, the Children's Media Foundation is considering the impact these unprecedented times will have had on the children's audience. There have been seismic changes in such a short time.

Lockdown, worldwide, has meant an expansion of media and screen use for children. Parents have to a great extent relaxed their concerns about screen time. Children and teenagers have turned to screens for learning more comprehensively than ever before. There has been wide foraging for new content on new platforms - music concerts in Fortnite, daily playdates with Joe Wicks on YouTube. Social media contact with friends has become not just normal but essential. For many there has been a host of new experiences both in media use and real-world engagement.

How much will children have given up in terms of their privacy? How much more dependent upon screen time will they be? How has their relationship with public service content changed? And how many more "unknown unknowns" are yet to emerge, both in their relationship with media and their real-world experiences and attitudes?

And that's just those who have access. There has been a stark contrast for children and young people in households with limited access. The crisis has laid bare the problem of the digitally disadvantaged and the Foundation will need to factor this into future thinking.

But the crisis has also put enormous strains on media production and freelancers. The knock-on affect for CMF is that our donations come from these sources and we can only hope that the industry will continue to support us because there is all the more need for the advocacy and scrutiny we offer during these uncertain times. Equally, the effects on the children's media industry – uncertainty and rapid change - may continue and it will need advocates in the form of trade associations and friends. The Foundation see itself as a "critical friend" – there to support initiatives that bring additional funding, or level the playing field with sensible regulation. Despite the strains on our finances we're going to stick around and the work continues.

Since the general election we have been able to re-establish the All-Party Parliamentary Group on Children's Media and the Arts. Our stewardship of that will remain a core activity and a powerful route to influence. Our Academic Advisory Board continues to guide and provide intelligence from the world of research. They will be a key source of advice and potential partnerships as we develop our report on the future of public service content for children and young people. In that task we'll take a comprehensive long-view approach to all the changes, pressures, and new sources of content, as well as new ways of viewing, using and even participating in media, that may be accelerated by the Covid crisis.

Meanwhile, our Executive Group continues to work to stimulate public discussion of the issues around children and media and we respond to consultations from regulators, government, and Parliament – including most recently comment on the decriminalisation of the Licence Fee and the BBC proposals to drop Newsround bulletins in favour of online content. You can see all our interventions and lobbying on the CMF website.

CMF's monthly newsletters will keep you in touch with not only our activity but also all the key trends and issues in children's media, regulation and policy, and despite it being difficult to produce a printed issue of the Children's Media Yearbook this year – this online version also covers many of the trends and concerns.

As for many charities and non-profit organisations, times are hard. But supporters are still coming forward. Two new Lifetime Patrons joined the ranks of Philip Pullman, Ant and Dec, Anne Wood, and Brian Cosgrove in support of CMF in early 2020. We are really pleased to welcome Maddy Darrell and Billy Macqueen from production company Darrall Macqueen. Their support has energised everyone who works in volunteer capacities for CMF to continue to pursue the best possible media for children in the UK, and ensure our activities are motivated and informed by research and reasoned discussion, and underpinned by a positive view of what the future holds for kids and the content they enjoy.

If you can help us by joining as a supporter or patron, or if your company can set aside a small amount annually to join the ranks of over 30 corporate supporters who back what we are doing, now would be a good time to come forward.

Become a supporter or a patron:
www.thechildrensmediafoundation.org

THE ISSUES AHEAD

ANNA HOME OBE
Chair, the Children's Media Foundation

The arrival of Covid-19 has had a life-changing impact on us, our children, and the media, and it will continue to shape our social and economic futures.

For kids, media has never been so important in terms of information, communication, education, and entertainment. It is crucial that this is recognised as future broadcasting policy is debated. There are currently two major policy topics under discussion which will impact on children and which concern CMF.

The first topic is the future of public service broadcasting (PSB) in the context of the ongoing rise of subscription video on demand (SVOD), the decline of advertising revenue for commercial PSBs, and the future of the BBC's role and funding.

CMF is pleased that Ofcom's intervention into the provision of children's content by the commercial PSBs, together with the companies' encouraging response to the Young Audiences Content Fund pilot, has the potential to lead to a real increase in original UK content. However, Covid-19 has disrupted the pilot timetable and delayed the evaluation process. There also seems to have been no public discussion of future funding beyond the pilot. Given the likely economic downturn caused by lockdown, and the inevitable pressure on budgets, this lack of discussion is worrying, and something CMF will pursue.

We are also concerned about pressures on the BBC. Despite the fact that the mid-term review is not due until next year, and charter renewal not until 2027, there is already a great deal of speculation around the future of the Corporation. It is important in this debate that children's interests are protected, and the continuing need for a wide range of properly funded content for all ages and platforms recognised.

CMF believes that these issues need to be thoroughly debated and researched. With that in mind, we intend to initiate (in partnership with others) an in-depth investigation into what the scenario for kids' PSB content might be in the future.

The second critical issue is that of online safety for children and potential regulation and legislation.

The need for some form of regulation to protect children online has been controversial but has recently become more accepted and progress has been made. On the 2nd September 2020 the Age Appropriate Design Code became law in the UK, this new Information Commissioner regulation means that any website, app or digital service with users or operations in the UK will now have to consider the best interests of their under-18 audience in designing their services. It's a big step in the direction of the "default on" position CMF has been campaigning for over the last few years. No longer reliant on parental controls, gateways or "walled gardens" to protect children under 13 from data harvesting or algorithms recommending inappropriate content, it enshrines the concept that the internet's default position should be an assumption of the duty of care for younger users.

However, at the time of writing, the

government's Online Harms Bill appears to be in limbo. It is important that this bill is passed and other international discussions continue about regulation and the responsibilities of online providers towards children.

CMF will continue to pursue these and other issues concerning children's media which arise in the next year; we will also support our colleagues in the industry who are under great pressure at present.

DO YOU WRITE SCRIPTS, BOOKS OR ARTICLES?

- ALCS is a membership organisation run by writers, for writers

- Since 1977 we have paid over £500m to writers

- Join 100,000 other writers in the UK and across the world and become a Member

Find out more and join online >> **alcs.co.uk**

AUTHORS' LICENSING AND COLLECTING SOCIETY
PROTECTING AND PROMOTING AUTHORS' RIGHTS

The Children's Media Foundation thanks

NICKELODEON

for their support for
The Children's Media Yearbook
2020

The Children's Media Foundation thanks

MILKSHAKE!

for their support for
The Children's Media Yearbook
2020

The Children's Media Foundation thanks

NIELSEN BOOK

for their support for
The Children's Media Yearbook
2020

Supporters are the grass-roots and life-blood of the CMF.

We need your support:
thechildrensmediafoundation.org

STATE OF PLAY

Children's creativity and development are strongly linked, and in 2020 play has never been more important; to discover, to create, to imagine and to express themselves. Children's Media gives them the tools but when opportunities for play are limited through circumstance, children will find a way and we celebrate their capacity to find joy and an outlet for emotions in challenging circumstances.

Photo by Robert Collins on Unsplash

STATE OF PLAY

CREATIVITY IS MAGIC, AND MAGIC IS FOR EVERYONE

CRESSIDA COWELL
Children's Author and Waterstones Children's Laureate

I have spent twenty years writing for children, and over those twenty years I have lost count of the times people have asked me, 'Have you ever thought of writing for adults?' as if writing for children was some sort of second best activity, something you do before moving on to the higher level of writing for adults. As adults we can get confused by trivialities. Children are focussed on the essentials.

I often get asked if I had ever wanted to move to LA and be a screenwriter for *How to Train Your Dragon*. The answer is no. I wasn't a film writer, I was a book writer.

I should pause here to say that I LOVE the work Dreamworks have done on *How To Train Your Dragon*. The most incredible team have worked on the movies – the producer, Bonnie

Cressida with HTTYD Director Dean Deblois

Arnold, the director Dean Deblois, the brilliant animation team, the music by John Powell… They have created something that's stunning, and absolutely in the spirit of what I spent 15 years writing. Every time I watch the films, I get emotional, not just because the end result is so spectacular, but because something so personal to me also became special to them, and that comes across beautifully on screen. I am grateful to them, beyond words.

But my own personal Quest is to create books and to play some small part in trying to get the children of today to read and write and draw with the same excitement and wonder that I did when I was a kid.

One of my own first rules about writing for children is that: THERE ARE NO RULES. Children are natural anarchists, so breaking the rules is going to attract them. I revel in language, I use buckets of similes and practically a metaphor a paragraph and I don't care if that's bad writing, if it's good enough for Dickens it's good enough for me, and wouldn't it be a shame if we ALL wrote like Ernest Hemingway or Elmore Leonard, wonderful though those writers obviously are.

At the beginning of writing *Dragon And Wizards*, I made the decision I'm going to write these books for 8 to 12 year olds and their parents and carers; books that get kids reading, that will be funny, clever, visually packed adventure stories that get kids thinking; books that will be written for everyone, mass market. And those choices I make at the beginning affect everything about the way I write the story and how I present it.

Not only is there hot competition nowadays for children's time and attention, books can also suffer from being perceived by children as something old-fashioned, 'school-y'. I work very, very hard to overturn that impression, and make sure that the stories are worth the effort the child has to put in to access them. The storylines are pacy, and thrilling, with lots of cliff-hangers and I pay a huge amount of attention to the visual aspect of the story. Even though these books are for older readers, I pack them with illustrations as if they are 350-page picture books.

I make the cover friendly and exciting, and preferably shiny and jewel-like, so that in the mind of the child they are 'sweets', not 'brussels sprouts'. The illustrations are deliberately child-

STATE OF PLAY

like and scrawly, and look like something the young reader could do them themselves, which is important to me because I want to get them writing as well as reading

I write the books to be read aloud, and that is a key factor in getting a child to read for pleasure. Books read to you in your parents' voice live with you all your life. Reading a book aloud is a shared joy, and sends an important message to the children being read to: books are important, books are powerful, magical things, that can make your dad cry, or your mum laugh, and have the sort of wisdom in them that can change your life. With reading-aloud in mind, I think about the books as a performance, and the mouth-feel of the words, the loudness or softness, or bellow-y ness of the characters.

And I never EVER dumb down. Children are natural philosophers, naturally curious, natural linguists. My job is to engage the questioning spirit of children, so these are the kind of questions I'm asking the kids in these little fantasy books about dragons and wizards: do we live in a world of determinism or free will? What makes a good parent? How should we look after the environment? Is it ever justifiable to go to war?

This all sounds rather grand, but I take a lot of care to present it as fun. Creating for children is often a balance between having the courage to take something silly and make it serious and meaningful, and taking something serious and having the courage to make it a bit silly. Studying at St Martin's taught me to stick to my guns because when everybody else stood up and said 'this is my project on Death', and then the next person would say, 'this is my project on the rise of Nazi Germany' and then I would have to present my own work on 'Mr Orange the Talking Carrot'. But, you know, the talking carrot can also represent something equally worthwhile.

When I was made Children's Laureate last year, my speech was titled, Reading is Magic, and Magic is for Everyone. I'd now like to expand that statement to: Creativity is Magic, and Magic is for Everyone. Children have an explosive enthusiasm, a need to express their ideas, and a talent for innovation that surpasses a lot of adults.

Creativity is not a 'soft-skill'; the creative industries made over £100 billion for the UK economy in 2018 and creativity is increasingly important in a complex world. Children need and deserve equality of access not only to books but also equality of access to the time and tools to develop their own creativity. In my Waterstones Children's Laureate Charter, I have a point that children at school have the right to be creative for 15 minutes a week. No Rules, No Marking, Just Fun.

Creativity IS magic, and we need every single child to grow up with creative skills, no matter what job they have. We should be proud of our creative industries, and part of my role as Children's Laureate is to champion how vital what we do is, and how important it is to all of us that the UK stays a leader on the world stage.

CHILDREN'S MEDIA YEARBOOK 2020

PLAY AND THE ART OF PLAYFUL COMMUNICATION

ASH PERRIN

Founder and CEO, The Flying Seagull Project

Dedicated to Sir Ken Robinson for his shining light of inspiration and willingness to challenge the norm.

Let's start from absolute square 1. What is play?

Play is the indigenous language of the child, and it is the simplest language there is. It demands total revelation, full throttle energy and absolute authenticity. Play requires that we don't hold back, we be present, and jump in with a big YES. Real play cannot have an agenda, a pressure towards specific output. Play does not mean creatively managing a child's time or delivering morals or educational messages disguised as a game. Play means opening your full heart, engaging absolute flexibility of mind, and letting go. If you are unable, or unwilling to look foolish, you cannot work with kids. Play only works if

we lose all ego and give full heart. The most valuable thing you can ever offer a child is 'you', mistakes, doubts, and clumsiness included. By being your full self it enables them to do the same and to understand by your honesty that not one of us is perfect.

Play is something that begins the second we are born with the first breath drawn, or the first steps you took. You stood up, wobbled a bit, fell down, laughed a bit, and tried again. Playing with the various ways to rise and the multiple options for falling. It is all play

Play is not competitive. It's not about when, or to what level the result of the game delivers. It's about the quality and immersive depth of experience. It's these 'in the moment' processes that allow the most powerful, confident and genuine expressions of self.

In play there's no such thing as 'good enough'. This doesn't mean there are no winners or losers, but that neither carries lesser or greater status. This impetus towards proper full hearted non-layered play placed immediately into a professional context, for children of all descriptions can radically impact those engaging with it.

I founded The Flying Seagull Project 13 years ago, an arts organisation sharing circus, play, music and dance with children in crisis all over the world. We have built circus tents in refugee camps all over Europe, opened a play centre in rural Romania, danced and performed magic into every school for disability in Ghana and much more. The reason I say this is not to boast (though we are proud), but to show that

in spite of the assumed severity of a situation there is still the urgent need, and in fact enshrined right to give a child a chance to play. In some situations we have seen first-hand children who are completely shut down or uncontrollably violent, unable to interact with others yet transformed in hours by the shared experience of play. It is flippant to disregard these experiences as a mere distraction for children in childhood. Play forms building blocks for life. With these blocks solid, a life can build to unfathomable heights, but without this strong base the opposite is true and long-lasting trauma and hardship can be the result. In the past decade and a half, we

have worked with almost 200,000 children in 23 countries in situations that don't bear thinking about. I can therefore say that real play and genuine playful interaction can literally make the difference between life and death.

We work with raw passion and storm strength energy and have for over a decade. Our energy never runs low, because in any sphere of life, if you are genuinely enthusiastic and passionate about your work you are not only better at it but can develop a limitless stamina. Maybe in some industries you can fake this, but not when working with, or creating materials for kids. They can smell a rat from 100 miles and though they are obliged to go along with it, the impact will be less significant. We must do better.

In this current world within the conceptual 'new norm', we are facing a huge challenge but also incredible opportunity to deeply examine and develop the art of playful communication. The past decade's increasingly tidal movement towards screens and digital interaction has, in my opinion, brought us close to crisis. We have seen games and digital media take on an ever-expanding role within our children's lives from ages ever younger. As an additional resource to play, this may be a good thing, but the notion that it could be a replacement or alternative to real play is a potentially dangerous and damaging idea. It doesn't have to be so, and I don't believe we are over the precipice yet, but immediate and a bravely honest assessment and re-evaluation of these digital media and their intrusive capacity within our homes and schools are needed. This brings me back to the opportunity the 'new norm' represents. I for one will not accept that this 'new norm' means a fight-less acceptance of a communication limit, instead I will see it as a huge challenge to be faced and worked through. I deeply believe that play and playful communication is the key, and we have a

chance now to use these resources to a fuller and more profound level at a time when they are urgently needed.

Why does this matter?

All of us begin as pure hearted children, thirsty for experience and excited by all the world's bounty. Too often somewhere along the way we can lose our confidence, or our SPARK. For all of us working within childhood development it is our duty to recognise this and make the change to enshrine play into all our systems

The result will be a generation able to problem-solve to a whole new level. A generation willing to break the mould and rebel against accepted norms, to playfully explore other options and innovate or create fresh new solutions. From the environmental need for industrial redesign and green/renewable

integration to educational reform, population expansion related crisis, medical development, agriculture, politics, global economic stability...the sky is the limit.

A generation that dares to think 'outside of the box', and with the light touch of experimentation and acceptance of failure offers an extremely exciting future.

So, what am I suggesting we do? How does this apply to you?

When creating anything that is targeted at communicating with children, we must always remember that how life feels matters. I'm lucky enough to be totally in love with my work and excited by every plan and project we make. If you're working with children in any capacity, you no doubt went into it with this same passion and joy. If you no longer feel that it is crucial you immediately seek out why and remedy it. In their early years, children absorb everything like hyper-sponges from outer space. Whether you are advising a distant board somewhere on content for exercise books in schools, or on the front line of social care remember that you have the ability and arguably the responsibility to use the fire and pure energy of your heart to encourage and light the paths of others. You are the inspirers, the magic makers, the knowledge sharers and soul lifters. Always remember that you can and must make a difference to every life you touch. Go forward and pour such passion into your work that the world is brighter for it.

CHILDREN'S MEDIA YEARBOOK 2020

WHAT'S IN THE BRIEFCASE?

DAVID KLEEMAN

Advisory Board Chair

International Children's TV Festival Prix Jeunesse

The PRIX JEUNESSE is the global children's television festival aimed at promoting excellence in television for young people, in particular for children to see, hear and express themselves and their culture, therefore enhancing an awareness of other cultures. It has been taking place in Munich every other year since 1964. Winning at PRIX JEUNESSE is the industry's top honor; participating in PRIX JEUNESSE is the industry's top creative professional development experience. .

The Prix Jeunesse regularly "exports" its insights and the content submitted to the festival through what has become know as the Prix Jeunesse Suitcase – originally a bag full of videos that organisations could watch and discuss as though they were virtual festival attendees.

In the UK, the Suitcase has become a regular feature of the Children's Media Conference in Sheffield. But 2020 was a particularly difficult year to choose programmes from the Prix Jeunesse to feature at the rapidly reconfigured

STATE OF PLAY

CMC 2020 Online. When choosing the programs to feature I've always had the benefit of the multicultural discussions in Munich. These give me insight into whether content that I found intriguing is also of interest to others. Of course, this wasn't possible this year. The PRIX JEUNESSE 2020 discussions took the form of interviews with the content creators, rather than open discussion among delegates from around the world, so my only guides were the questions filed in chat before and during those interviews.

In the end, we opted to place three "briefcases" in the Children's Media Conference on-demand catalogue, instead of one longer session. This created an opportunity to link shows with similar themes and explain each collection in a video introduction.

Winners, Close to Home, and Memories of WWII

Everyone is interested in the festival's winning programmes, so one briefcase had to be filled with these. In a globalized world of content, PRIX JEUNESSE is one of the few places to see content made uniquely for a particular country or region, so "local" content packed the second briefcase. Finally, 2020 was the 75th anniversary of World War II's end in Europe, and three finalists' programmes dealt with children's unique, harrowing experiences of the war and its end, providing a one-time opportunity for exploration of methods of storytelling and approaches to sensitive content.

Close to Home

I've long been fascinated by children's content made for a particular place, and especially shows where the landscape of a country becomes a character in itself. In the Briefcase, I featured two Argentine shows. *Clorophilia* from Canal Encuentro explores the country's diverse ecological regions, with each episode done in the style of a particular filmmaker. Easy access to drone videography enabled soaring shots of tall trees and wide landscapes, and extreme close-up cameras focused in on tiny plants. *Sound Hunters* from Pakapaka, by contrast, featured children recording the natural and man-made sounds of Argentina. Both programmes centered children in their own land and celebrated what makes it special. As the one-time head of children's programming for Danish public broadcasting, Mogens Vemmer, used to ask his team, **"when children wake up in the morning and turn on the TV how do they know where they are?"** Children's worlds grow in concentric circles – home, block, neighbourhood, city, country, world – and TV can play a critical role in expanding their reach beyond their experience.

Memories of War

Three shows commemorating the end in Europe of World War II went into this Briefcase: *Kids of Courage* from Germany and *Chika: The Dog from the Ghetto* both from Germany, and *The Star of Andra* and *Tati* from Italy. Each focused on the closing days of the war, but that was the only commonality. Two were set in concentration

Kids of Courage

camps and one in a Jewish ghetto. One was stop-motion puppetry, one was animated, and one was live action. One told the story of sisters separated from their parents in the camps, their survival to liberation and reconnection with their mother, plus a concurrent story of skeptical current-day teens visiting the camp and hearing their story. One combined drama and documentary footage to follow a young woman who survived the camps by singing for the guards but felt the guilt of being unable to save other members of her choir. The last used remarkable objects – German books and newspapers, for example – to create the "scenery" in a dark puppet story of a boy's separation from his beloved dog, when his Jewish family went into hiding in a secret basement shelter.

Chika The Dog From The Ghetto

This is a great illustration of the power of PRIX JEUNESSE. There are infinite ways to tell stories, and the festival is a treasure trove to compare and contrast, whether across topic like these three, or around genre, style, age, culture and more. While the shows aired initially on different channels, in two different countries, it was a powerful reminder that we are children's window into the big world and the scope of history, as well as their mirror on the moment in which they live.

Winners

The winners at PRIX JEUNESSE are chosen by scores assigned by delegates. Anyone participating in the festival can register as a juror. Moreover, even the top-rated programme's average score needs to be above a certain minimum to earn the prize. This means that an entry has to gain the favour of a diverse group of registrants, across geographic and cultural spans, and professional strands (writers, producers, executives, educators, researchers). There is a children's jury for the middle age groups (7-10 Fiction and Non-Fiction) and an International Youth Jury for the oldest category (11-15), and it's always fascinating to see how the professionals agree with (seldom) or differ from (usually) the kids.

The 2020 prize in Non-Fiction for the 11-15 age group went to the World War II story of the young singer, featured in the other briefcase – a mix of narrative and documentary. In the briefcase at CMC, I featured a Norwegian show for under-twos that gave lots of space and time to toddlers being themselves (Non-Fiction Up to 6); a French animation about an owl lost in a bayou hurricane (Fiction Up to 6); an Australian schoolyard comedy with a fantastic deadpan kid actor in the lead (Fiction 7-10); a simplest-possible format from the Netherlands with a barber engaging his tween-age customers in conversation, and getting remarkable life stories and challenges from them (Non-Fiction 7-10); and

STATE OF PLAY

Shooom's Odyssey

a raucous and profane comedy about growing up Black and Somali and poor in Norway (Fiction 11-15).

Aside from overall quality and delightful viewing, initially it appears hard to draw a common theme among the winners. This too is one of the pleasures of PRIX JEUNESSE. Whatever you've come in search of, you can likely find it – laughter or tears, the shock of the new or a unique twist on a classic, a kids-eye view of a primetime genre or the answer to a question that only a child would ask. However, one theme is common throughout and that is 'change'. 2020 has been a year of change for everyone accelerated by the unusual circumstances we find ourselves in. Every 'next' generation seeks change, and so it is with this year's Winners as this generation becomes more involved in shaping what content they like to see, creating it themselves, or how it's delivered. The animation of the owl in the hurricane (*Shooom's Odyssey*) reflects a cause the young are passionate about; climate change. And finally, war changes everything – especially for children.

It was a pleasure to present the briefcase screenings to the "Still Here, Right Now" Children's Media Community, but I really missed hearing the instantaneous reactions to the innovative and challenging works; it felt a bit like chord progression that never resolves. Let's cross fingers for a 2021 CMC in person, where I promise to present more gems from the PRIX JEUNESSE!

STATE OF PLAY

Children's nonfiction book-buying is diversifying, both in authorship and in subject matter. The latest data from Nielsen Book Research shows a continued increase in both the numbers of titles available and the volume sales of factual books for children, and within this there is a continued broadening of the subjects that are proving popular..

The children's general nonfiction category is distinct from that which houses game tie-ins (Minecraft, Pokemon), branded product (Lego, League Of Legends), and other 'leisure' titles, such as joke books. We can, therefore, examine the category's performance to see the underlying trend for factual books without being impacted by large spikes produced by the latest kids' craze.

In 2019 there were 25,000 different titles in the UK market in this category, which has doubled in value over 10 years to £22.3m today. This growth has been steady since records began in 2001 and can be seen relative to growth in the overall children's market in the following graph of print book volume sales over time.

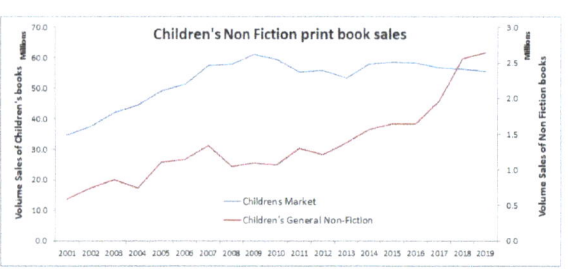

If we then look at the most popular subjects in nonfiction as a whole in 2019 (Graph 2), we can see that a number of 'core' subjects, such as history and maths, remain popular (note that this category does not include school textbooks), as well as less mainstream subjects such as wildlife and poetry. The latter genre has shown a particular boost in recent times with top titles, including *A Poem for Every Night of the Year* by Allie Eseri and *I Am the Seed That Grew the Tree: A Nature Poem for Every Day of the Year*, which have lifetime combined sales of 100,000 copies.

Among the top genres in 2019 is that of Personal & Social Issues, an umbrella for a number of sub-categories, including Self-awareness & Self-esteem, Body & Health, Family Issues, and Racism & Multiculturalism. Most of these nonfiction categories have seen an increase in sales in the past few years; though, of course, this won't be reflective of the entire catalogue available as many of these issues are dealt with in children's fiction and picture book titles, such as those shown in Picture 3

If we look at the largest sub-categories in Personal & Social Issues over the last five years, we can see that the long-term trend shows growth (Graph 4). In 2019, the bestselling children's nonfiction book was You Are Awesome: Find Your Confidence and Dare to Be Brilliant, by Matthew Syed, selling 68.8k copies, which contributes to the large spike in Self-awareness & Self-esteem in 2019, and in 2018 (the year it was published) when it also topped the same chart, selling 139.2k copies.

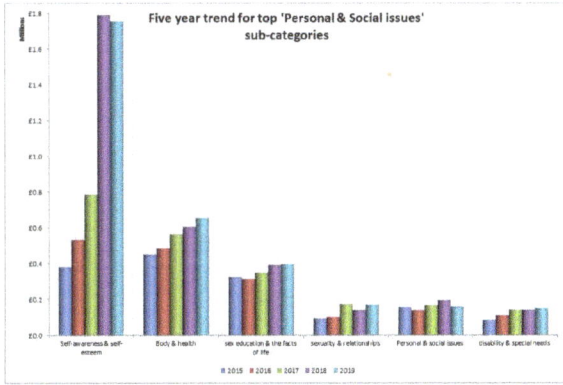

This category has seen several high-profile titles sell in large numbers, but the growth has also come from strong performances in the list outside of the bestsellers (Picture 5).

If we look at these titles, we see they deal with a range of topics. Some give children the confidence and empowerment to try new things, something that perhaps the adults in their lives aim to do but don't always get right. Other books explain changes children may be undergoing physically and mentally, or address anxiety and worries by helping them make sense of the world around them. The reviews of these bestsellers indicate that the key to a well-received book appears to be hitting the correct tone, explaining in a non-patronising way, and making the subject matter fun.

These books tend to be purchased predominantly by females, who have accounted for 65% of purchases of Personal & Social Issue titles in the last couple of years; this is in line with purchases of children's books overall. We also see that 53% of Personal & Social Issue books are bought for a female end-user. This is the converse of what we see for general nonfiction children's book purchasing, where 61% of titles were bought for a male end-user.

The success of titles in this category shows an increasing awareness among adults (who write, publish, market, and sell these titles) of the need for books aimed at younger people that address these types of subjects. It also mirrors the trends present in the adult market. Personal development as a theme is present across a number of categories, with guides on being happy and healthy in both mind and body performing well, as shown in Graph 6.

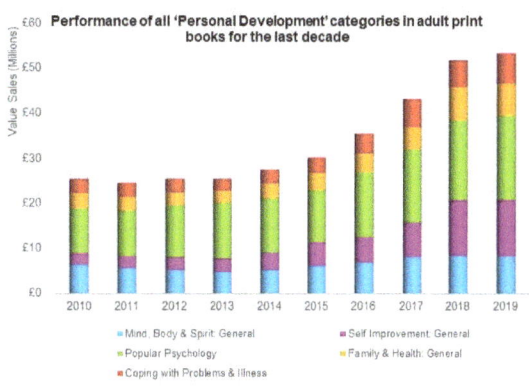

Interestingly, we see a number of books dealing with self-awareness and self-esteem that have been around for many years, such as one of the 2019 bestsellers: *What to Do When You*

Worry Too Much: A Kid's Guide to Overcoming Anxiety, by Dawn Huebner. Although this title was published in 2005, it sold 15,361 copies in 2019 and was the 12th bestselling nonfiction book that year. If we look at the top titles in Personal & Social Issues in 2019, we find 64% of the value sales of these books were from titles published before 2018, which is even higher than for nonfiction books in general. This compares with the balance between older and newer titles in the category of Children's Fiction, for example, where 46% of the value is from sales of older titles. So, older or 'backlist' titles have more than half the market share, showing the longevity of books written on this subject.

In the top 100,000 bestselling nonfiction, we also see the increasing presence of book titles containing keywords such as 'anxiety' (included in 44 book titles in 2019, compared with 19 in 2015), 'worry' (24 titles in 2019, compared with 13 in 2015) and 'esteem' (30 titles in 2019, compared with 23 in 2015).

If we look to the coming year, nearly 1,000 titles are due to be published with inspirational or positive messaging that have been given a Personal & Social Issues label. These range from *The Amazing A-Z of Resilience* by David Gumbrell, and *Big Ideas for Little Philosophers: Equality with Simone de Beauvoir* … some heavy-hitting titles which I think us grown-ups could do with reading!

CHILDREN'S MEDIA YEARBOOK 2020

THE BUNNY FROM BROOKLYN
BUGS BUNNY'S 80TH Birthday
—

As Over the past eighty 80 years, Bugs Bunny —known as a "wascally wabbit" by his fellow Looney Tunes character, Elmer Fudd —has entertained audiences of all ages with his zany antics and endearing, timeless appeal. Bugs Bunny's long ears, knowing eyes, snappy smile and trademark buck teeth are iconic, but it's his street smarts and charismatic character that have endeared him to fans across the globe.

STATE OF PLAY

First created in 1940, Bugs Bunny quickly stood out as an internationally recognised symbol of the Looney Tunes franchise, and Warner Bros. Animation. In an era when cartoon stars were cute and innocuous, Bugs Bunny dared to be different with a quick wit, a brains-over-brawn attitude and an unflappable demeanour, which continues to make this no-nonsense bunny from Brooklyn, New York favourite.

Simultaneously timeless and timely, Bugs Bunny graces screens of all sizes, from television and movies, to phones and tablets. He also lends his likeness to a range of consumer products, allowing fans to integrate the animated celebrity into their everyday lives. Continuing his reign into the twenty-first century, the universally recognised leader of the Looney Tunes squad is more popular than ever, attracting new generations of fans, as well as delighting long-time devotees.

A few words from the Executive Producer of Bugs Bunny, Pete Browngardt:

"Bugs Bunny is the character so many of us dream to be. He's the smartest guy in the room. Stands up to bullies, winning every time. And knows the perfect thing to say given any situation. What's not to love?"

"I feel very lucky that I have this opportunity to add to the amazing rich legacy of Bug Bunny. He's one of the major reasons I fell in love with animation as a kid and why I became an artist. I have to pinch myself daily."

20 Bugs Bunny Facts

1. Bugs Bunny is from the east side of New York City and speaks in a signature Brooklyn accent.
2. Bugs Bunny made his official debut on July 27, 1940, in Tex Avery's *A Wild Hare (1940)*.
3. The most popular rabbit in the world was first named Happy Rabbit, before being renamed Bugs Bunny after his original writer Ben "Bugs" Hardaway.
4. Talents include opera singer, baseball player, pianist and, of course, trickster.
5. After having appeared in the 1943 *Super-Rabbit* in U.S. Marine Corps dress blues, Bugs Bunny was named an honorary Marine Master Sergeant.
6. Bugs Bunny earned a star on the Hollywood Walk of Fame in 1985; he is the only Warner Bros. animated character to have a star
7. In 1997, Bugs Bunny became the first cartoon on a U.S. postage stamp.
8. Bugs Bunny's personality and mannerisms are inspired by Charlie Chaplin, Groucho Marx and Clark Gable, among others.
9. Mel Blanc voiced Bugs Bunny for nearly fifty years, and his legacy has been carried on by just a small handful of actors, including Jeff Bergman, Billy West, Joe Alaskey and Eric Bauza.
10. Mel Blanc actually ate carrots while voicing the iconic character.
11. *The Bugs Bunny Comic Strip* ran for almost fifty years, from 1943 to 1990.
12. *What's Opera, Doc?*, the 1957 short featuring Bugs Bunny and Elmer Fudd, was the first cartoon to be selected into the National Film Registry in 1992.
13. Bugs Bunny has been delighting audiences with orchestras around the world for over Thirty years as the star of *Bugs Bunny at the Symphony*.
14. The *Bugs Bunny Show*, which debuted on ABC in 1960, was a network television staple for over forty years.
15. Bugs Bunny, trickster that he is, has only been thwarted by four other characters in eighty years.
16. Bugs Bunny's missed left turn at Albuquerque has brought him to such far off locations as Mexico, the Himalayas, Scotland and Germany.
17. Bugs Bunny has appeared in over 175 theatrical shorts, more than any other animated character.
18. Bugs Bunny has been nominated for three Academy Awards, and won - in 1958, for *Knighty Knight, Bugs* (with Yosemite Sam).
19. Bugs Bunny appears in theme parks in many countries, including the largest indoor theme park in the world: Warner Bros. World, Abu Dhabi.
20. Bugs Bunny is a master of disguise and has confused his enemies as a barber, a policeman, a baker, a gentleman, and of course, the beautiful Brunhilde.

FRIENDS

We all need a friend every now and again, and to children and young people they are increasingly important in 2020. Family might be all to very young children, but making friends is an important part of development and finding out who you are. To young teens, friends are everything as they look for ways to express their individuality while staying part of a group. What does the rise of prominent friendship groups mean to providers of Children's Media?

KIDS MEDIA WORLDS RIGHT NOW

MAXINE FOX
Managing Director
Giraffe Insights

The daily ritual evolves as we do

We have seen over the last 3 years within Giraffe Insights' 'Kids and the Screen' research, and in over 70,000 recorded viewing occasions, that kids consume content in a ritualistic manner across the day. There are viewing peaks before the school day begins and when children return from school, with the pre-school audience viewing more consistently throughout.

Across lockdown, we tracked viewing to see how this ritualistic behaviour evolved or changed. We identified a routine and a pattern, but one which had evolved to mirror the new day that had formed. Consequently, viewing had increased overall and had become far more consistent across the day, with time of day when content was consumed being impacted by different needs ignited by being at home.

The early morning slot pre-9am that was previously dominated by live TV shifted, with kids getting up later to begin their day. The demand for online content in the morning had increased, with platforms such as YouTube providing educational and gaming content to keep kids occupied. For the rest of the day subscription video on demand (SVOD) platforms dominated, as parents started their own working day, relying on platforms they deem safe with content that will engage their child for a longer period of time. As we venture into the

FRIENDS

late afternoon and evening, we saw family viewing becoming more frequent with many indulging in movie nights on a regular basis.

[Consumption throughout the day chart: Before Lockdown vs During Lockdown across Early morning (up to 9am), Late morning (9am – 12pm), Early afternoon (12pm – 3pm), Late afternoon (3pm – 5pm), Early evening (5pm – 7pm), Late evening (7pm onwards)]

New needs came to the fore

Prior to lockdown the need for content that satisfied a learning objective along with being entertaining for children was a trend that was increasing. Within our 'Little Voices' study we can see that this further increased over the lockdown period with this type of content providing more guilt free screen time for parents and acting as a support for at home learning with kids absent from the classroom.

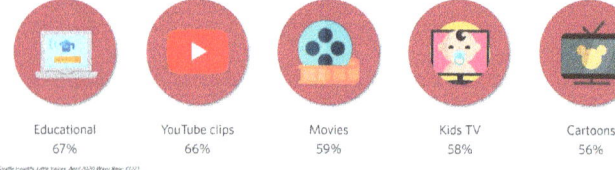

What type of content is your child now watching more of?
- Educational 67%
- YouTube clips 66%
- Movies 59%
- Kids TV 58%
- Cartoons 56%

Another need which was strengthened over the lockdown period was that of family time and the need for family entertainment. Across multiple recent studies that we have conducted, parents have indicated that one positive to come from these difficult times is that they have been able to reconnect as a family and have taken part in activities together. When cinemas closed their doors, at home film nights became the perfect way to do this. With families re-connecting and taking a step back from the 'everyday' many remembered just how important time together is and this a need which is likely to continue as a result.

The continued climb of SVOD

SVOD viewing has gradually increased over the last 3 years, rivaling that of live TV and this has only been exacerbated by the recent lockdown period.

As a result of new needs emerging, we have seen some real winners in the kids' and family content space. With Disney+ making a timely release as we entered lockdown it provided families with exactly what they needed– new and fresh content that they can watch together. Within our 'Kids and the Screen' research we can see that Disney+ satisfies a different need to the biggest player in the SVOD space for kids, Netflix. Whilst Netflix is often watched independently by children, with episodes of shows dominating, Disney+ is watched by the whole family and primarily for films. Disney+ is not only fulfilling the family need, but it is also doing this when other SVOD platforms are not.

Navigating back to the future

So, with this in mind, how will viewing be impacted more long term?

The educational need that has been increasing in popularity over the last year is likely to continue Its success. We have seen Joe Wicks supplementing PE lessons during the lockdown period, and whilst lockdown specific content such as this is likely to decline, educational shows we see prior to lockdown will continue their rein. Currently, SVOD platforms such as Netflix and online platforms such as YouTube are working the hardest in this space for families when it comes to this need for 'edutainment'.

SVOD will continue to be a favourite way to view for kids and families, with Disney+ satisfying the family entertainment need. Disney+ and Netflix can co-exist, complementing each other on content needs, however there is a question over whether households will eventually become overwhelmed by subscriptions and need to reduce household outgoings – in this instance only the strongest will survive!

It's evident from our 'Kids and the Screen' and 'Little Voices' research that there are viewing behaviours that represent a snapshot in time in response to these unprecedented circumstances and others which will be here to stay as we navigate back to the future. It's important for brands to consider what's going on right now and where this is heading particularly as we approach the fourth quarter where strategies need to be informed rather than predicted to ensure greatest success.

FRIENDS

THE RISE OF THE 'VLOGGER NEXT DOOR'
Ofcom's Making Sense of Media research

JESSICA REES
Children's Media Literacy Research, Ofcom

Children's viewing landscape is constantly evolving. What are their current content needs and how do they fulfil these? How important is it that content reflects their lives? Ofcom's research provides rich insight into the evolving nature of children's viewing landscape, with a particular focus on their content needs and the platforms they use to meet these. We explore what content children are most attracted to and why.

Media literacy enables people to have the skills, knowledge and understanding to make full use of the opportunities presented by both traditional and new communications services. Ofcom has a duty to promote and research media literacy and we carry out a range of studies to understand this area better. We call this research: Making Sense of Media.

One of our key pieces of research is our annual quantitative **Children and Parents' Media Use and Attitudes Tracker**, which provides detailed evidence on media access, use, and understanding among children aged 3-15 (and their parents). And another, is our **Children's Media Lives** research, a qualitative research project which is designed as a way of providing a small-scale, rich and detailed qualitative complement to Ofcom's quantitative surveys of media literacy.[1]

Key findings from our 2019 research in relation to children's evolving viewing landscape

More children watch video-on-demand (VoD) than watch live broadcast TV

Eight in ten children aged 5-15 (80%) watch some form of VoD content – doubling from 44%

---

[1] For more information about our children's media literacy research and for links to all of our research reports: https://www.ofcom.org.uk/research-and-data/media-literacy-research/childrens

in 2015.[2] By comparison, three-quarters of 5-15s watch live broadcast TV[3], meaning a quarter do not watch live broadcast TV at all. Viewing of VoD content increases with age, ranging from 65% of 3-4s to 88% of 12-15s in 2019, while viewing of live TV is comparable among all age groups.

Children are spending less time watching broadcast TV than before

Figures from BARB (the UK TV audience measurement body) also show the overall decline in broadcast television viewing by children on the TV set.[4] Viewing among children aged 4-15 declined in 2018 by over an hour since 2017; and the first half (H1) of 2019 saw a continuation in this decline[5] – down from 8 hours 59 minutes a week of consolidated broadcast TV in 2018, to 7 hours 56 minutes in H1 2019.

Children shifting to smartphones and tablets to watch TV content

The proportion of children watching TV content on a TV set has decreased to 91% (from 94% in 2018 and 96% five years ago). Meanwhile, the proportion of 5-15s using mobile devices to watch TV programmes or films are increasing, and at a faster rate than the decline in watching a TV set; 43% now use a tablet for this purpose (compared to 33% in 2018), and 26% use a mobile phone (up from 20% in 2018).

Older children especially are shifting to mobile devices for their viewing needs. Forty-two percent of 8-11s and 46% of 12-15s now use a tablet to watch TV content (up from 30% and 35% respectively in 2018).

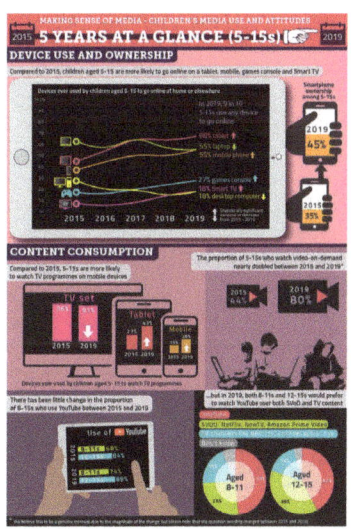

Attitudes towards representation in TV programmes vary across the UK[6]

There has been a decrease since 2018 in the proportion of both 8-11s and 12-15s who feel there are enough programmes that show children who live in the same part of the country as them; from 53% to

---

2   We believe this to be a genuine increase due to the magnitude of the change, but please note that the question wording changed between 2015 and 2019.

3   Trend data is not available for VoD vs. live TV due to a change in the question wording in the 2019 survey

4   Broadcast television viewing is seven days consolidated viewing, including live, catch-up and recorded content on the TV set.

5   At the time of reporting, the full year of 2019 data was not yet available from BARB

6   Ofcom highlighted its concerns about the lack of programmes that enable children to see themselves on screen in its Children's Content Review. We expect the commercial public service broadcasters' subsequent renewed commitment and new investment from the BFI's Young Audience Content Fund to improve the availability of programmes that better reflect young people's lives from across the UK. Ofcom's Children's content review.

FRIENDS

42% for 8-11s, and from 48% to 41% for 12-15s. When asked if there are enough TV programmes[7] for children their age, two-thirds of 8-11s and 12-15s say that there were – although this is down since 2018 for 8-11s (from 73%).

Children in Wales and Northern Ireland are less likely to feel there are enough programmes for children their age, or that show children from the same part of the country as them. It is also more important for both nations that there are enough programmes that show children from their country.

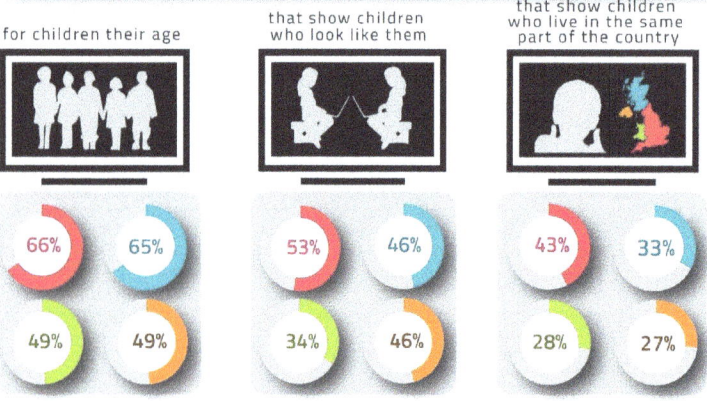

Differing views by UK nation of representation in programmes

Proportion of 8-15 year olds in England, Scotland, Wales, and N Ireland who believe there are enough TV programmes...

for children their age	that show children who look like them	that show children who live in the same part of the country
66% / 65%	53% / 46%	43% / 33%
49% / 49%	34% / 46%	28% / 27%

YouTube remains firm favourite over TV or on-demand content

Used by three-quarters of 5-15s, YouTube remains a significant player in the panorama of children's viewing. This is particularly true among older children; nine in ten

---
7   Based on children watching TV at home or elsewhere – therefore, this could be on any device or platform.

12-15s say they use the YouTube site or app. YouTube is now also used by half of children aged 3-4; up from 45% in 2018.

When asked if they could pick only one platform to watch, 45% of 5-15s chose YouTube – a higher proportion than those who chose on-demand, such as Netflix (32%), or TV channels such as BBC and ITV (17%).

...because it gives children total control and choice over what they watch

Children are drawn to YouTube for a variety of reasons, and it varies by age. Cartoons and animations continue to be the most popular content among younger children (3-7s), while watching funny videos, pranks and music videos are more popular among older children.

And, YouTube has increasingly become the 'go-to' place to find out about hobbies and interests. In 2019, more than half of internet users aged 12-15 (55%) said they would go to YouTube first to find accurate and true information about fun activities – a significant increase since 2018 (38%).

Several children in our Media Lives explained they preferred the content available on YouTube to that on live television or subscription-video-on-demand (SVoD) services such as Netflix because it gave them more choice over what they watched and was less "random" than live television. For instance, Zak, 10, said he found there was more content on YouTube that aligned to his interests, such as the YouTuber, Dan TDM.

And some children felt YouTube was more relatable and authentic

A number of children in our Media Lives indicated that they felt YouTube content was more relatable and authentic than the perhaps more polished content on other platforms. For example, William, 15, said that he preferred YouTube over Netflix because "it's made by normal people". He particularly liked "commentary channels" where he could watch content producers watching and reacting to other videos they found online, such as the YouTuber JaakMaate.

The rise of the 'vlogger next door'

Almost half of 12-15s and more than a third of 8-11s watch vloggers or YouTube influencers, although 2019 has seen a shift in the types of people they are watching.

A key finding in our 2019 Media Lives study reveals that, while children remain keen on big-name YouTube 'stars', they are also following an increasing number of peer-to-peer[8] or local influencers – known as 'micro' or 'nano' influencers (i.e. people with tens or hundreds of thousands of followers rather than millions). This shows they value being able to follow the lives of people in their local area, or those with similar interests to them, and perhaps gain more direct engagement with these influencers than their more-established or 'celebrity' counterparts.

---

[8] 'Peer-to-peer' influencers tended to be less well-known names with smaller followings and sometimes more niche interests.

FRIENDS

BIG STEPS FOR LITTLE RADIO

CHRIS JARVIS

Little Radio DJ and CBeebies Presenter

The term 'Anorak' was coined by Radio Caroline's Andy Archer back in the '60s to describe over enthusiastic fans who sailed out to see the pirate ship. Imagine! There's no way I'd brave the North Sea in the vain hope of catching a glimpse of Andy or Tony Blackburn on a rocking boat, but if you watched Children's BBC in the 90s, you'll know that I'm a bit of an anorak because as well as loving my job on children's TV, I am obsessed with radio.

A dream came true last October when I helped launch *Little Radio*, a brand-new station playing a simple format of nursery rhymes and children's songs with stories at bedtime. It's like a commercial 'hot hits' station for pre-schoolers – instead of Little Mix we play *Little Bo Peep*. There's only positive news, the music is always happy and our weather forecasts go no further than saying "it might be chilly so do up your coat!" It's an introduction to the concept of radio with jingles, DJs and hourly time checks, although you're more likely to hear ducks quacking the hour than the GMT pips.

Please give us a listen and let me know what you think! The Little Radio app is free to download and you can take us anywhere.

Getting fresh material from other contributors has been relatively easy; if they haven't got a home studio or podcast mic, the microphone on a smartphone sounds great and their only real challenge was finding a reverb-free room to record in. Many storytellers have shone torches under the duvet to record wonderful reassuring tales for Lockdown for us, one favourite is *The Rabbit That Wanted To Play* told by Jan Francis.

Soon after the Lockdown began, *Little Radio* was commissioned to make the *CBeebies Magic Den* for BBC Sounds and CBeebies Radio. The idea is simple: I'm hanging out in a magically ridiculous den with Stuffy (a toy from CBeebies *Show Me Show Me*) and Aunt Edie (an homage to the late great Thora Hird). We get in touch with a celebrity friend who chats about their farfetched den, then takes us on an Alice-like journey to a land of make believe; Maggie Aderin-Pocock from CBeebies Stargazing took us to a planet of unicorns and Dr Ranj from *Get Well Soon* shrunk us to the size of an atom for a tour of the body.

Episode Four:
CBeebies Magic Den 'Planet of the Unicorn'
with Chris Jarvis & Maggie Aderin-Pocock

We had to be equally creative with the technology. One triumph was when Jennie Dale (who plays Captain Captain in *Swashbuckle* on CBeebies) sang a song using a smartphone for foldback and a tablet as a recorder – once again, all under the duvet! Her pitch perfect performance was emailed over and pieced back together in the studio.

Throughout Lockdown listenership for all radio rocketed as everyone searched for breaks from screens. With so much learning pushed on-line, radio has given children another form of entertainment not connected to nursery or school. It is a medium that ventures wherever it wishes, using words and sounds to conjure up incredible pictures in young minds. It improves listening skills no end and provides a familiar voice to connect the listener to the outside world - so important when stuck indoors. For content producers, Radio's simple processes mean consistent and fresh shows can be produced remotely. Is it any wonder that Radio is having a moment?

For the occasional break from screens, please check out our wee station and podcast.
Chris Jarvis   @LittleRadioUK
https://www.littleradio.co.uk

CBeebies Magic Den
https://www.bbc.co.uk/programmes/p08dhlpt

MODERN FAMILY

If friends become family, what does family mean in 2020? How we see society is another area of rapid change and young people think of inclusivity and diversity as an important part of who they are as a generation. They support climate change, Black Lives Matter, disability and gender issues and are leading the way in changing attitudes. Children's Media Foundation have always campaigned for children's and young people's right to inclusivity and diversity in the media, and now young voices from those groups are breaking through.

Daniel cheung-unsplash

BLACK LIVES MATTER;
What Does It Mean for the Children's Media Industry?

ZOË DANIEL
Writer and Multimedia Journalist

It goes without saying that the past six months have seen change and difference like never before, with "unprecedented times" becoming the buzzword of the year. Alongside the pandemic, we've seen the Black Lives Matter movement grow in global prominence. For People of Colour and particularly, the Black community this has been more than a movement for change, but the reality of existence for many years before this.

Children's Media holds the privilege but also the responsibility to ensure that all young people see themselves in the media they consume, that all children have access to media they can relate to made by creatives that share their lived experience to effectively make media that's accurate, current and doesn't rely on tired stereotypes. And in the new climate, that this representation goes beyond performative gestures and stirs constructive change not only for the young people consuming, but also those creating. It won't happen overnight, but it starts now, and with us all, especially those at the top and with the allyship of White colleagues too.

CMC 2020 rebuilt its schedule to include an unprecedented "opening keynote panel" to attempt to provide insights into what a more inclusive future for children's media could and should look like. The views below are taken from that discussion between some key actors in the movement for change.

Jacqueline Baker: BAME Task Force

The main concerns expressed were the importance of gatekeepers and ensuring that those creating content from on-screen to off-screen, editorial and commissioners, reflect the UK and/ or the community they are creating content for. This was highlighted by Jacqueline Baker who is co-founder of the BAME TV Task Force. The Task Force sprung up amid the Black Lives Matter movement and is lobbying for fundamental change in the television industry to stamp out racism and improve representation for diverse storytellers on-screen. The Taskforce articulated practical steps major broadcaster and media content creators can implement in order to actually create positive change.

The important of recognising truth was also a concern raised by Professor Kevin Clark. Professor Clark is a children's media consultant based in the US, who recently published in Kidscreen Magazine "How to move beyond tokenism in kids' TV". He contends there can no longer be a debate about the existence of racism and systemic oppression simply because white colleagues in the industry have not experienced it or don't see how as an issue it presents itself systemically. The children's media industry has a responsibility to provide children and the next generation with agency and to see themselves as agents for change – this was articulated by Larissa Kennedy who is currently President-elect at the National Union of Students.

It's also interesting and worth examining the reaction from children to the movement and how they feel as members of society and the audience in which we make media for. There's no denying young people see themselves changing the world and but furthermore this generation are taking ownership of the world they live in by becoming leaders of change, from Greta Thunberg to Amika George.

Amika George

In terms of the video gaming and online industry, it was thought-provoking to note what Adam Campbell Director of Product at Azoomee and Co-founder of the organisation POC in Play had to share, as it varied in nature to what was discussed regarding other parts of the media scene. Adam highlighted that the gaming industry was younger than other children's media sectors, despite being the largest entertainment industry in the world - exceeding sport in recent years - and so had more work to do. In terms of staffers, there is less diverse workforce making the media, which could also mean fewer People of

Adam Campbell, Azoomee

Colour as consumers because the stories do not reflect different types of people. And considering the gaming world often explores more fantastical storyworlds, how are aliens portrayed, or People of Colour in stories set in the future?

The importance of having diverse People of Colour in positions of creative decision making was highlighted in relation to recognising that there are differences within Black and other ethnic groups. People of Colour often become one dimensional characters in the media because creative decisions aren't encompassing the variety and difference that occurs within minority groups themselves. One Black face in a company can't tick the diversity box, there's got to be a team from various backgrounds in control of creative decision-making in order to present an authentic and nuanced portrayal of all communities, It also requires those making creative decisions to consult with a variety of People of Colour to achieve accuracy and quality of content. Children who are Black or Mixed Race or Asian will all have variance in their lived experience of racism and it's children's media responsibility to reflect that. Miranda Wayland, Head of Creative Diversity at the BBC took this a step further by expressing that it's also children's media practitioners' role to understand that People of Colour are more than their experience of racism and their skillset and areas of interest can range far beyond the pigmentation of their skin. ?

Larissa Kennedy, with an educational perspective, asked who is training the next generation of media creators? Who do people of colour breaking into the industry have to look up to? How do media companies reach these creatives from minority backgrounds? Having a senior creative in a position of power championing and mentoring People of Colour off-screen will have a significant impact on that Person of Colour's ability to progress and reach those gatekeeping roles that have creative control over what content gets made and how it gets made.

This panel at the Children's Media Conference was the best attended of the whole event. What delegates took away was that there remains a level of uncomfortableness when it comes to discussing race, a fear of saying the wrong thing… but that is ok. The advice - let that discomfort drive you to seek out what you can do in your practice to make children's media a place where children of every background can feel they are seen, heard, understood and championed.

Willingness to commit is the first step to creating a more inclusive future.

MODERN FAMILY

IS THIS OK?

LUCY EDWARDS
Radio 1 Presenter and YouTuber

This is me aged 6
Little sighted Lucy had no idea back then her 24 year old self would never see her own face again.

This girl dreamed of being a presenter, someone who made a difference and changed the world. She had no idea how much she would go through back then - in such a short space of time.

Sighted Lucy never had any doubt she could be anything she wanted to be. The world would look at her and believe that she would amount to something great. But that girl, eventually, through no fault of her own, found herself in a sighted world not made for people like her anymore.

When I was younger, because I was sighted, I was incredibly lucky. I saw people like me on my favourite programs. It cemented my belief in myself and my ability. If they could do it - I could. *Bamzooki* was one of my favourite shows. I would spend hours with my sister creating my *Bamzooki* fighting creature online in the hope it would be featured on CBBC. Those memories, however happy, are tainted. Knowing that someone else, the exact same age, through no fault of their own, was not able to enjoy that same activity upsets me. Not back then. Not now. Because they are blind.

800,000 children in the UK have a disability. 1 in 20. According to the Disability Living Foundation.

The Creative Diversity Network's latest Diamond report released earlier this year found that 7.8% of people on screen and 5.2% off-screen are disabled. 18% of the working age population are disabled. We have a long way to go.

Those are the overall stats but in children's media it's not a lot better. In 2018 the CDN found 5% are on screen and 9.3% off-screen.

Now in 2020 the on-screen representation is at 6.2% and off-screen 5.7%. Overall disabled representation has decreased in children's media.

Is this ok?

Before I acquired my disability, I had never thought about disability. Is this ok? Disability isn't mainstream.

Is this ok?

By age 17 I had lost all useable vision I once had and I was scared. Never having seen anyone else like me what an earth was I going to do? I felt ashamed to be who I was and I had spent the last few years dying my hair every colour under the sun because media perpetuated stereotypes led me to believe that caring about my hair and makeup wasn't going to be important anymore if I lost my eyesight.

On 23rd March 2013 I sat in a dimly lit eye hospital ward and my world faded to black. Trauma and shock set in and my life was different in an instant. The grief hit me like a ton of bricks.

These emotions were inevitable but what made that period of my life even more impossible was the idea that blind me was somehow more broken and less valid. I am not able anymore. I'm disabled. I'm an inspiration, not a leader. I am a curiosity not a talent.

That first year I would walk like a zombie to the shop with my guide dog on the days I could muster up the energy only to be confronted by a well-meaning person telling me I am an inspiration for picking up a tin of baked beans. Something clicked deep inside of me that day. I started reading headline after headline that inferred that I was a burden. Watching program after program that didn't have audio description. It was and still is relentless. You just learn

MODERN FAMILY

to block it out for a while.

A few months passed and my YouTube channel was born. If I added to the conversation I thought, surely, things will definitely change. My video 'blind girl does her own makeup' went viral. I was so excited. I felt so empowered. However, the comments involved 'bless her', 'she can so see - no blind person can do their makeup like that' and 'omg!!!!'.

The weight of the world was on my shoulders. I cried myself to sleep that night. Tired. So tired. I will never be equal or valid, I thought. I had no role models so I made myself one. No one helped me navigate blindness. There was no guide book.

I picked myself back up and found my true love for the media world. I started to block out the comments because I was learning my new normal. Uploading to the internet allowed diverse voices to be heard. But we're still a way off inclusion.

Presenting and storytelling are two things that make me feel the most Lucy. It fired up a new energy in me that was so exciting. I applied for the BBC's Extend in Digital News scheme. It was a really sunny day and I sat on the sofa in my parents dining room and my phone started ringing. It was Ian George informing me that I was now a BBC journalist. I cried tears of joy because I could not only tell my story but other people's. These are the types of schemes that will change the landscape of our industry for the better. It will lead to true inclusion when disabled journalists entering the industry become presenters, leaders and commissioners on big shows. Shows about everything and anything. A diverse voice is a valuable voice. It changed my life. Katie Lloyd, Sarah Lambley and Ian George are change-makers. They are disability allies. Is this you?

I found true acceptance of myself and my disability when I said that my voice was a valued voice. My work and campaigning taught me to be unapologetically me. I became the first ever blind presenter on BBC Radio 1 in December last year.

I could not stop smiling when I found out. 17-year-

old Lucy would never believe there would be this amount of acceptance and change happening in her lifetime. I am now working with BBC engineers to make at least 1 of the 60 London studios accessible and it feels like we are making some small steps towards true inclusivity but we still have a way to go. There is still a long way to go before true inclusion for disabled talent. What can you do? Become a disability ally.

Have an expectation on your disabled colleagues. Involve disabled colleagues, talent and actors to have a creative input on every project. Increase disabled talent on and off screen. Pledge today that this will be a priority for you in 2020 and beyond. Don't be afraid to include us for fear that you may offend. This creates a bigger divide and now more than ever we need representation. If disabled children don't see themselves on their TV screens, they will just feel more isolated. In a world where you don't see yourself represented why would you believe that it is a viable thing you could achieve when you are older?

Normalising disability is key and this is what I work to do every day.

Follow my work:
TikTok: https://www.tiktok.com/@lucyedwardsblind
YouTube: https://www.youtube.com/lucyedwards
Twitter www.twitter.com/lucyedwards
Instagram: https://www.instagram.com/lucyedwardsofficial/
Website: https://www.lucyedwardsofficial.com/

MODERN FAMILY

MISSION EMPLOYABLE: PRESENTING POPULAR SHOWS IN BSL

CECILIA WEISS

Digital Producer, iChild and CMF Executive Group

"You can't be what you can't see". Inclusivity for children's media means children are featured from different walks of life, ethnicities, cultures, class, gender identity, physical ability, etc. allowing every child to feel represented in the programmes and videos they are watching and hearing. Today's generation are much more accepting of difference than previous ones. However, while there's plenty currently being written about a range of issues, the needs of visually and hearing-impaired children are often overlooked. We had "*Something Special*" with Mr Tumble on CBeebies for young children using Makaton, and BBC's "*See Hear*", which serves the wider British Sign Language community, but little more. Until the advent of "*Mission Employable*" and "*Dare Master*", two very successful series on CITV, presented by a charismatic teenager, whose first language is British Sign Language.

Both these series were made by SignPost Productions which is ITV's centre of excellence for multi-platform British Sign Language services. SignPost combines industry-leading expertise and resources with a passion for social mobility and diversity.

In 2016, SignPost was commissioned to make a mainstream kids' series that was fully accessible for Deaf children. Their secret: look through a pool of talented young people whose first language is BSL, select a top presenter and come up with a couple of fantastic programme ideas. The result was the previously mentioned *Mission Employable* and *Dare Master*, two of the most popular shows on

Gareth Deighan

He believes that genuine inclusion in programmes is paying dividends for them. Without this commitment, Danny Murphy, now an award-winning presenter, may have been overlooked. He said diversity is essential not least because working hard to find the right people, from whatever background they come from, gives you the great opportunity to find undiscovered talent who bring with them new and different perspectives.

Christopher Luke

Christopher Luke, producer at ITV SignPost Productions and Sign Language Services, and series producer on "*Mission Employable*" and "*Dare Master*", thinks you need to take into account a mixture of deaf and hearing people when working with a bi-lingual team. Making more accessible content with more inclusive teams is not difficult, and SignPost are happy to share

The main aim of both programmes was to be great entertainment; great entertainment presented in British Sign Language. They brought British Sign Language into the mainstream, normalising this different form of communication for all children.

Viewing figures for both programmes were good. Dare Master's peak saw 83k individuals watching, 67k of them being children.

And when the shows repeated in lockdown, Dare Master had a 5.1% average share of child viewers.

Gareth Deighan, ITV SignPost Productions' Head of Content, leads the production team.

their knowledge and experience of what works well and less well. There are adjustments to make; but not adjustments that would prevent using an inclusive staff. Adjustments that, when they're made, become the norm and give access to undiscovered talent.

Danny Murphy is the presenter of both *Mission Employable* and *Dare Master*. His first language is BSL, which he believes needs more

MODERN FAMILY

Danny Murphy

recognition as a language and that it's so important to have deaf presenters on TV. Many children often recognise him now, whether or not they use BSL. As Danny says: "People need to know about the deaf community and how that's reflected in our language and culture. When it comes to being a presenter, deaf people can do it!"

CHILDREN'S MEDIA YEARBOOK 2020

REMEMBER, REMEMBER: THE TWENTIETH OF NOVEMBER:

United Nations Convention on the Rights of the Child

JAYNE KIRHAM

Writer

Did you know World Children's Day is celebrated on 20 November each year? Me neither. Last year's World Children's Day was particularly special because it marked the 30th Anniversary of the United Nations Convention on the Rights of the Child (UNCRC).

What is the UNCRC? It's an agreement made up of "54 articles that cover all aspects of a child's life and sets out the civil, political, economic, social and cultural rights that all children everywhere are entitled to. It also explains how adults and governments must work together to make

MODERN FAMILY

sure all children can enjoy all their rights" 1(UNICEF).

Given that the UNCRC is the most widely ratified human rights treaty in history[2], can anyone remember celebrating it in November 2019? Me neither.

I hate missing celebrations but it's ok, I've found another: 2021 will be the 30th anniversary of the UK signing up to the UNCRC. Hooray!

But does the UK have anything to celebrate? Signing up to something is not the same as implementing. Implementing 54 articles takes time, apparently, so UNICEF UK regularly monitors the country's progress. In July 2016 UNICEF UK welcomed the UK's measures to address child sexual exploitation and abuse, its new legislation on human trafficking and the decreasing use of exclusion from school. But it also criticised "recent fiscal policies and allocation of resources" that had contributed to inequality and meant children in disadvantaged situations were disproportionately disadvantaged.[3]

When asked in Parliament how Government was addressing these criticisms in 2019, the then Under-Secretary of State for Education, Nadhim Zahawi, announced an assessment template to help staff across government give "due consideration" to the UNCRC when making new policy and legislation.[4] In effect, putting young people at the heart of all policy.

Putting young people at the heart of all policy? Come on, that's pretty fantastic!

Yes. But. In the same year, one year ago, evidence from 100 charities and academics presented, not a fantastic but pretty devastating picture[5], one that left UNICEF UK "deeply concerned". In fact, UNICEF said that "While the Government continues to focus on Brexit, it is not addressing impact on children's rights issues, such as the rising number of children in poverty, school exclusions and the rise in

---

1   https://www.unicef.org.uk/what-we-do/un-convention-child-rights/

2   192 out of 193 UN Member states has ratified the convention. The only nation that has not signed is the USA.

3   Committee on the Rights of the Child, Concluding Observations on the Fifth Periodic Report of the United Kingdom of Great Britain and Northern Ireland, 3 June 2016.http://www.crae.org.uk/media/93148/UK-concluding-observations-2016.pdf

4   https://hansard.parliament.uk/Commons/2019-06-24/debates/C07550C9-C069-4AE7-93BC-5EB65270CB91/UNConventionOnTheRightsOfTheChild

5   Children's Rights Alliance for England, State of Children's Rights 2018, March 2019.

mental health diagnoses amongst young people." This means that children's fundamental human rights, such as their right to a clean environment, to a home and a safe place to live, their right to play and education, and their right to be protected from abuse are being side-lined."[6]

That's pretty damning. Given the political landscape of the past few years, this new Government can't blame anyone else for this, there's nothing pretty about it, damning indictment. They are going to have to pull all fingers out of wherever they've stuck them to make things right.

Even so, the UNCRC doesn't just speak to Governments: all adults have a part to play. Those involved in children's arts and media especially. Several of the UNCRC articles speak directly to what we do: children have:

- a right to freedom of expression, to seek, receive and impart information and ideas through any medium (Article 13)

- a right to mass media that ensures information from a diversity of sources that promotes their social, spiritual and moral well-being as well as their physical and mental health (Article 17)

- a right to education that contributes to the elimination of ignorance and illiteracy throughout the world (Article 28) while also helping the development of their personality, talents, mental and physical abilities to their fullest potential (Article 29)

and my favourite –
- the right to rest and leisure, to engage in play and age-appropriate recreational activities and to participate in cultural life and the arts (Article 31)

and my favourite bit of my favourite article?
- Governments shall respect and promote this right encouraging **"the provision of appropriate and quality opportunities for cultural, artistic, recreational and leisure activity."**[7]

Which means things like public service broadcasting, arts council funding, the animation tax break, the licence fee, the Young Audience Content Fund, public libraries, VAT exemption for books, regulatory bodies, are essential if the Government is to fulfil the commitments of all these articles.

Yes, radiotherapy equipment is a higher priority than a roundabout

---

6   5 UNICEF, 'New Report Finds Little Evidence of Progress on Children's Rights Issues in England— UNICEF UK Responds', 12 March 2019.

7   Article 31:1 https://downloads.unicef.org.uk/wp-content/uploads/2010/05/UNCRC_united_nations_convention_on_the_rights_of_the_child.pdf?_ga=2.151558713.1291592115.1584005635-409452386.1583823287

MODERN FAMILY

but the UNCRC articles "have equal importance."[8] Mass Media, Education, Culture and the Arts help **"prepare a child for responsible life in a free society, in the spirit of understanding, peace, tolerance, equality and friendship among all peoples"**[9]. This is nothing new. Content created specifically for children has been doing these things for far longer than 30 years. But what the UNCRC did was give universal recognition of the value of such content - "equal importance." That we, the people that create this content, use our talents and skills to fulfil these rights of the child, now that is worth celebrating, don't you think?

---

[8] https://www.unicef.org.uk/what-we-do/un-convention-child-rights/

[9] Article 29 https://downloads.unicef.org.uk/wp-content/uploads/2010/05/UNCRC_united_nations_convention_on_the_rights_of_the_child.pdf?_ga=2.151558713.1291592115.1584005635-409452386.1583823287

STRANGER THINGS

Traditional TV and viewing habits of children and young people are changing rapidly, and the events of 2020 are to a certain extent dictating the pace. Digital Channels, SVOD, tablets and phones mean the audience are not only choosing what they want but how they want it delivered. There is also a growing trend towards self-produced material. The Children's Media Industry must stay one step ahead of the game in order to keep up.

puneeth-shetty on unsplash

UNDERSTANDING CHILDREN'S SVOD HABITS

HELEN LOCKETT
Research Manager, Discovery

RYAN LEWIS
Research Manager, BBC Children's

The children's media landscape is ever changing, especially with the growth of established Subscription Video On Demand services and regular addition of new ones to the mix. Discovery Channel worked with the BBC to understand what children aged 0-16 years choose to watch and why – and what this means for SVOD platforms and content providers.

There has been a dramatic shift in the children's media landscape within the last few years, from linear TV to streaming services such as Netflix. This shift has impacted how, when and where children are consuming content, and their expectations of the type of content they want to consume. Children's increased viewing during lockdown also makes this a crucial time to understand these habits. Although our research was conducted prior to the Covid crisis, the drivers we identified are still clearly present.

We spoke to 35 children across the UK, all aged between 0-16 years, using a cumulative process of passive tracking, a video diary, online community and in-home interviews. We found that SVOD (Subscription Video On Demand) is watched more than live TV – across our two weeks of passive tracking, our sample of 35 children watched a collective 2.5 days' worth of Netflix and almost 13 days' worth of YouTube! This backs up the simple but dominant fact that SVOD services have an important place in children's lives. Even before the age of 3, children are gaining control over what they watch – although generally within parent-approved services. SVOD services give children this freedom.

Who chooses the content that they are viewing?

> "He asks for his favourite shows about 90% of the time, the rest of the time we will pop something in for him"
> Male, 2 years old

So how can you attract children to your content in this market? We have identified 6 key things you need to know.

1. There is a tension between usability and content

For younger children (under 5yrs), usability is more of a barrier to usage than content. There is a wealth of great content out there, with many beloved shows on BBC iPlayer. However, if the service isn't easy enough for them to navigate, you'll lose them to competitors like Netflix.

For older children, particularly the 6-9 years age range, great content becomes harder to find and so the balance shifts. Give them the content they're looking for, and they'll manage to navigate a less intuitive platform.

2. Younger children are savvy navigators – they use characters to find what they are looking for

Children in general tend to navigate services on the homepage instead of using the search bar. 0-5 years identify shows by character, not by title or logos/screenshots from the show. This means that having recognisable characters in your show, and using these on the homepage rather than episode stills, makes navigation much easier for this age group.

Younger children also like bright backgrounds and fun cartoons – although parents still want the shows to have some educational aspect to them! A colourful main character attracted our youngest sample most. It makes it easier for them to find your show.

3. Kids want content that reflects who they are

For all ages, humour and fun is important – it's particularly key for keeping kids over 6 years interested in your platform and content. But what kids really want to see in content is representation: seeing people that look like themselves, and seeing their interests represented. YouTube is particularly strong in this, given their huge range of creators and content.

Nevertheless, children tend to project upwards, often watching content that is aimed at a slightly older audience to their own age – this holds across the full age range of 0-16's, and is often most pronounced when a child has older siblings. They want content that feels more grown up, and aspirational without being completely age inappropriate.

4. It's about keeping content together, not separate

Children are no longer bound by scheduling. Instead they choose content based on their need states, e.g. mood management or social cache. They also don't think of content as based on brands or sub-brands (or channels), so they don't expect to look for content in different places on a SVOD service.

Instead, they expect personalisation, and for all the content relevant to them to be served up on the homepage. They're happy for it to be categorised on the homepage, but don't want to have to move between pages – in fact, it doesn't even cross their mind to try.

5. Families will share logins unless prompted otherwise

For the BBC, the question of logins was key. Personalisation is so important, but it doesn't work properly if it's reading a whole family's preferences instead of one person. However, we found that unless prompted and really easy, like Netflix's profiles, families don't switch logins between members, leaving personalisation muddled and children at risk of seeing adult content.

Personalisation also extends to profile details – kids felt more encouraged to use logins and more personal ownership if they were able to

customise their profile to reflect themselves, e.g. changing their profile picture or name.

6. A walled garden which grows with kids will win

We know personalisation is essential, as is showing content that helps kids feel more grown-up while still being age appropriate. While several SVOD services have these elements, what few, if any, services were doing is growing with the child throughout the entire 0-16 years age range. Effective walled gardens often need to be toggled on/off, and are set to younger content that may lose kids as they become older but not yet old enough for the full adult range of content.

A service that can grow and adapt to kids would therefore win – having an effective walled garden for the youngest children that expands as children grow older without having to manually change settings would be a huge asset. But it may be a few years away!

The BBC's perspective

So far, we've been able to use this research to really allow us to hone in and start to focus our activity on iPlayer in the right places to most efficiently improve things for children.

For the youngest children we had the award-winning iPlayer Kids app already which was well received by the audience, but there was an acknowledgement that the improvement in user experience had to be bigger and broader across the whole of iPlayer (if not the BBC). We've built on both our content offer and platform usability to better suit their needs and expectations.

Our wonderful UX&D (User Experience and Design) and Profile teams have worked with the Children's department to create a method of both account creation – and then after that account switching – which brings down the barriers to entry and the barriers to continued use. We've now got children's profiles on TV and are continuing to invest our time and effort into the offer here.

The original process that was delivered for children to create a BBC account just wasn't friendly enough at launch for them – and their parents – to sign up to it. What barriers seemed fairly logical and practical on paper – with responsibilities to the audience in mind – turned into something of a confusing and frustrating process when rolled out at scale. This research really helped to clearly highlight just how big a gulf there was between the ease of use and perceived experience on other platforms compared to our own.

We've really changed how iPlayer presents programmes to children. We've done all we can to make it more accessible for children whose language skills aren't as developed, focusing less on the words and more on the visuals. iPlayer for children's accounts is much brighter, more colourful, with more familiar characters and a selection of family viewing scattered amongst the other titles. Children are able to easily navigate between CBBC, CBeebies and safe content from the wider BBC, and clearly choose between them when they choose iPlayer – making a far better first impression when they arrive.

By combining a broader range of shows with more image led navigation, all on the back of an increasingly personalised presentation, we're joining things up to make iPlayer more child friendly than ever.

STRANGER THINGS

6 EXPERT TIPS FOR PRODUCING INTERACTIVE TV SHOWS

KATE DIMBLEBY
Co-founder and Producer, Stornaway Productions

IAN LIVINGSTONE CBE
CHAIRMAN
SUMO GROUP, PLC

AMY GROSSBERG
SERIES PRODUCER
9 STORY MEDIA GROUP

ALEX BREEN
VICE PRESIDENT OF INTERACTIVE
9 STORY MEDIA GROUP

EMMA EARLE
CO-ARTISTIC DIRECTOR
PINS & NEEDLES PRODUCTIONS

DANIEL EFERGAN
EXECUTIVE CREATIVE DIRECTOR
OF INTERACTIVE, AARDMAN

MATT BRANDON
SERIES PRODUCER
PLIMSOLL PRODUCTIONS

RACHEL DRUMMOND HAY
MANAGING DIRECTOR
DRUMMER TV

TIM WRIGHT
ACTING HEAD OF IMMERSIVE
NFTS

This article is a digest of a video we created for the Children's Media Conference 2020 that explored a new trend in interactive storytelling on TV.

We asked top writers, producers and heads of interactive to share their thoughts on the revival in the form and their insights about writing and producing interactive TV.

> "Whenever I say I work in interactive storytelling, people say, 'Oh, is that the thing where you get to decide the ending?' — that's what people think it is — and I say, 'Well... sort of...'"
> Tim Wright, acting head of immersive, National Film and Television School

Interactive storytelling comes in many forms. But what is this new wave of interactive TV that can be found on streaming platforms? In particular being pioneered by Netflix, following the success of

CHILDREN'S MEDIA YEARBOOK 2020

Charlie Brooker's interactive Black Mirror episode *Bandersnatch*

Is it TV or is it a game? We interviewed 8 writers, producers and heads of interactive about these new types of TV shows.

We spoke to them about the future of interactive storytelling and asked them to give us some tips when writing and producing interactive film and TV stories. Here are 6 of their top tips

IAN LIVINGSTONE CBE
CHAIRMAN, SUMO GROUP PLC

1. Make choices have real consequence

We asked games industry grandmaster and co-creator of the legendary 1980s *Fighting Fantasy* game books, Ian Livingstone, about what makes a good branching narrative:

> "The most important thing when writing a branching narrative on whatever medium it is, is that choice has to have real consequence, otherwise it's pointless. I've seen some offerings where it doesn't matter if you choose A or B, you end up at the same point. People think, "That's pretty boring" — you have to have consequence for your actions."

2. Tell a story that's enjoyable to watch and replay

It's not enough to just add on interactivity to linear stories. As Dan Efergan, head of interactive at Aardman Animations told us:

DANIEL EFERGAN
CREATIVE DIRECTOR OF INTERACTIVE, AARDMAN

> 'I think the best creative outputs (which is why I believe things like Bandersnatch have shone through) relate to each other linearly — so your experience at the end is related to your experience at the beginning — but also 'across': so if you play it once and you play it again and go for another choice, those both relate to each other as well.'

3. Don't hesitate, just jump in!

Matt Brandon, a producer for Plimsoll Productions is currently developing an interactive

MATT BRANDON
SERIES PRODUCER, PLIMSOLL PRODUCTIONS

63

format for a streaming platform, using Stornaway. He told us about using the new tools for interactive storytelling:

> "It was a constant learning curve and a really fun one to go on — and something I hope to do more and more again. My advice would be roll your sleeves up and jump in and have a go at it. Have a play, it feels like playing a game, it's really fun."

4. You don't need to know how to code anymore

TIM WRIGHT
ACTING HEAD OF IMMERSIVE, NFTS

Tim Wright, acting head of immersive at NFTS has worked with interactive storytelling for a long time.

> "I think people feel it's a real high bar to get into interactive stuff because you've got to learn how to sort of programme — or at least not be sniggered at by people who know how to programme, but I think that's completely the wrong approach. I think you've just got to go out there with whatever skills or tools you've got and try it."

5. Test a lot, and create opportunities for exploration and discovery

AMY GROSSBERG
SERIES PRODUCER, 9 STORY MEDIA GROUP

Amy Grossberg, series producer for 9 Story Media Group and Emmy nominee this year for *Blue's Clues and You Interactive*, talked about their rigorous iterative and collaborative creative process

> "There's a lot of testing that needs to be done and you need to be building that into your process. It's not just taking a regular linear schedule, duplicating it and making that for interactive. You need to leave beats and the opportunity for exploration and discovery"

6. And finally: pick a genre — any genre

Don't let your imagination be limited by what you've seen already. It's still very early days, and Amy Grossberg is really excited about the future of interactive shows, like *Unbreakable Kimmy Schmidt* – a Netflix TV series that premiered an interactive special in May 2020.

"This is really just the beginning of interactivity, in the way that we're exploring it now because there's more devices out there, there's more creators who are curious. Just thinking about how things could evolve with horror, drama, theatre... I think that there's just still so much potential out there."

STRANGER THINGS

LIVE THEATRE FOR KIDS
How Digital Can Make A Difference

NATHAN GUY
Actor and Drama Coach

In this world turned upside down by the Coronavirus much has been altered. There is a very relevant fear that our children are having a part of their childhood stolen by the Coronavirus pandemic.

In the midst of the fear and the unknown that the pandemic brings, I see opportunity. A way to do things differently. To continue to find different ways to share our experiences and the stories of others. We can continue to broaden young people's understanding of themselves in terms of hopes and aspirations for their future. Right now, young people need us more than ever: the arts are the missing link. A way to bridge the gap. From fear to understanding. We can utilise the arts to support young people. The truth is that there is nothing on earth so valuable as supplying children with the nourishment that they didn't know they needed.

Lyceum Theatre. Theatre has the ability to remind us we are not alone: it helps us to escape reality. As an audience member, you become intrigued about the lives and story lines of the characters; you laugh with them, cry with them and feel with them. You forget about what is happening in your personal life for a couple of hours and enjoy looking into the life of other people. It is the same for actors too who escape from reality to become somebody else and tell their story.

CHILDREN'S MEDIA YEARBOOK 2020

There is a plethora of research boasting of benefits associated to teaching the arts: taking an active part in theatre has proven to be beneficial which reinforces its importance in schools today. Teaching in one of London's hub schools, I have seen some of the biggest smiles on the faces of the young actors with whom I work with - especially in these trying times. For young people, being able to relate to and embody a character with completely different circumstances to their own, enables them to enjoy their own creativity through empathy and understanding. Through drama, young people can act out problems, talk candidly about worrisome topics, and remain in a safe place.

Before the pandemic, we were concerned about the detrimental effects of the digital world can have on children, but ironically the advantages of digital during lockdown is that it has provided a conduit for social support. We access streamed performances in the comfort of our own homes. Whilst a theatre visit isn't possible, access to theatrical productions from companies like The National Theatre and Lloyd Webber's Really Useful Group are available with a click to bring delight and relief to anxious audiences of all ages. This in turn keeps the interest in theatre alive, so that when the lockdown is over, the appetite to see live performances for real will still be there. It has the power to introduce theatre to groups of young people who may not normally choose to access live theatre for any number of reasons, from disadvantaged backgrounds to peer pressure.

Post Lockdown, it is regrettable that theatres are amongst the last places to reopen fully. But when they do, the audience's desire to be entertained will not have changed. Children will need the arts more than ever - especially after months of being isolated at home! This will see theatre do what theatre does best - creating a connection and immediacy you don't get on-line; allowing an audience to get lost in a story without interruption from the outside world - specifically your phone; bringing family and friends together for a shared experience. And thrilling entertainment.

Long live theatre and live storytelling! No matter which form it may take in today's world.

67

STRANGER THINGS

CREATING CONTENT FOR KIDS AND TEENS WITH 2020 VISION

PETE MAGINN

Director of Insight, Beano Brain

It's clear that 2020 is a year like no other. Family life has been turned upside down and nothing has been "normal". As a result, media has never been more important for kids and teens. It has been an essential part of their lives with multiple roles - to entertain, alleviate boredom and to both keep them connected or provide much-needed escapism.

In 2020, gaming has become even more important for so many kids. And we want to debunk the myth that still exists in many adult conversations about gaming being mindless screen time. Animal Crossing, Fortnite, Roblox, Minecraft - before lockdown, these were just computer games for kids. Now, they have become the virtual playgrounds for an entire generation, key for communication, friendships and happiness and a channel that has been particularly fascinating to explore throughout the pandemic.

Generation Alpha and Generation Z are a digitally-savvy group. They are pre-disposed to hack tech for their own purposes and, as lockdown progressed, we saw them evolve gaming from an entertainment platform to an essential tool for communication. As kids struggled to talk to their friends through video calls without shared experiences, the ease of being able to chat whilst playing games led to gaming becoming the new virtual playground.

There are 2 million kids aged 7-14 in the UK. In the first week of lockdown 60% of those we spoke to agreed that keeping in touch with friends made them feel better about the virus. But one month on, how they kept in contact had evolved. Initially, FaceTime and WhatsApp video dominated (42% had used each of them) but a month later, platforms that allowed them to play together and chat were seeing huge growth.

For example, by April, over a third (39%) of 7-14-year olds were connecting with friends each week via gaming app Roblox. XBox Live use had increased by 6% from March and a quarter (25%) had connected with friends using Houseparty in April, compared to only 9% in March

Gaming has proven that it is a multi-faceted and a crucial vehicle for, yes, play and entertainment, but also connection, escapism and socialising. A virtual autonomous space where kids and teens can hang out even when there are severely restricted physical options.

However, their online behaviour also changed. Kids and teens place huge value on family time and that has only increased this year. Looking at pre-pandemic data, to strict lockdown and then the restriction easing period, we've seen massive changes around the peaks and troughs of when kids are online. Most notably in both the UK and US, after school 5-9pm was the peak period of activity. That curve has now been flattened as we see kids going offline for dedicated family time at this time.

As families have spent more time together, TV has been at the heart of it. In late April, at the peak of lockdown, nearly half (46%) of kids and teens in the UK and US wanted more great shows to watch with their family.

STRANGER THINGS

When asked how they like to watch content, on-demand platforms such as YouTube, Netflix and Disney+ top the list in both the UK and US – and have collectively increased in preference by 15% from January to July 2020.

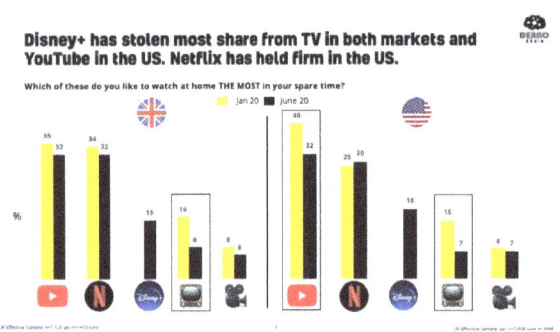

However, our Beano Brain research found that fewer than one in five 7-14 year olds in the UK and US think the people they see in TV shows and movies reflect their real lives. Despite several reviews across the globe, kids and teens are still not seeing the diversity of their reality in the content they watch, and teens are much more likely to identify the gap. Only 13% of 13-14-year olds in the US and 17% in the UK agree content reflects real life vs. 30% of 7-8 year olds in the US and 31% in the UK.

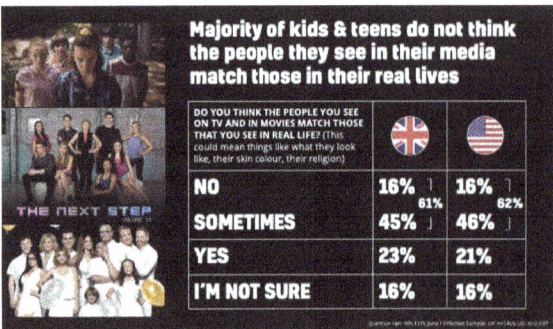

In the wake of the global Black Lives Matter protests, it's clear that diversity matters more than ever to this emerging young generation of consumers. Our insight work has clearly identified how frustrated kids and teens are with the adult world and are astonished and upset that adults and institutions discriminate.

Kids and teens actively pursue mainstream diversity. They judge people by who they are, not what they are. This is best reflected in the distinct gap in attitude towards gender between parents and their kids, with 32% of parents feeling their child's gender doesn't matter, compared to 58% of kids. Knowing this, it's little wonder that kids and teens seek content without stereotypes and that encompasses a variety of races, religions, sexualities and genders.

Kids and teens are savvy consumers and they have a huge amount of influence in the home. And as the personal and economic effects on families play out – with potential job losses, harder financial times surely coming, this generation will turn to media more, as they are much more aware of what is going in the world and in their own home than their predecessors.

In such massively challenging times, kids are more than ever before seeking escapism and some laughs. There is huge opportunity for media brands to help bring some light relief and really bring families and different generations together. Ways of communicating and connecting are changed forever. On the video learning, there have been a few success stories during the crisis from some brands that were already in the space but there is huge scope to make this more exciting, sophisticated – especially for this hugely visual generation.

Kids and teens look for positive role models and cues to help them qualify their experiences and feelings and negotiate complex issues. So, they seek their stories and lives reflected authentically in the content they consume. We shouldn't underestimate this young audience. They're not afraid to ask the salient questions and are increasingly ready to stand by what they believe in. One in five of those aged as young as 5 to 9 years-old have already been on a march or protest for something they care about. They are growing up in a time which will forever impact all of our lives. We owe it to and are expected by them, to tell stories which authentically reflect their lives

Beano Brain is tracking the behaviours and sentiments of kids, teens and their parents to identify and assess the impact of the unprecedented global events of 2020. It aims to help brands understand and better engage with families right now, as well as prepare for the future.

STRANGER THINGS

A PURPOSEFUL FUTURE

BRUNA CAPOZZOLI
Creative Director, Popcorn Digital

Brooke Cagle at Unsplash

Millennials, those aged roughly between 26 and 40, and Generation Z (11- to 25-year-olds) now make up over half the world's population. Gradually taking over senior positions in the media industry, they also represent the majority of a highly-skilled tech workforce. They are the ones behind the most successful start-ups, and they are the new parents. The Deloitte Global Millennial Survey 2019 calls them the 'Generation Disrupted', characterised by a lack of faith in traditional societal institutions, governments and business leaders, as well as a growing dissatisfaction within their own lives, financial situations, jobs and social media.

On a global scale, the rise in populism, the climate emergency and the economic obsession with growth that has been failing the vast majority while serving only a few, have jointly nourished an overall sense of uneasiness and discontent; reasons why Millennials and Gen Z, are, therefore, taking it upon themselves to design a purpose-focused culture for business, consumption and social experiences.

In 2018, the first wake up call for our industry came in the form of Greta Thunberg. At the age of 15, she became the ultimate symbol of climate activism. Though many indigenous, black, and brown youth activists, such as Jamie Margolin, Mari Copeny, Xiye Bastida, Isra Hirsi, Kevin J. Patel and Elsa Mengistu had also been working tirelessly on to championing the same cause. Nevertheless, content makers responded to Thunberg, and we are now about to witness a new boom in eco-conscious content aimed at kids. But these new 'green shows' are only a tentative attempt to retain relevance. Real transformation requires inner change, and the time has now come for companies to assess their values and the impact their activities have on the world around them.

The reality is that the perception about what a company actually stands for is already disrupting business, workforce, strategy and investment. The ways in which capital is raised, how success is measured, how businesses are structured and how key talent is hired and retained, are changing. The traditional capital-focused mindset is being replaced by new metrics, such as environmental impact, a company's mission and people policy.

Back in 2016, a survey titled *The Business Case for Purpose* drafted by a team from the Harvard Business Review Analytic Services for the EY's Beacon Institute, declared that "companies able to harness the power of purpose to drive performance and profitability enjoy a distinct competitive advantage."

In 2018, investors put US$1bn into purpose-driven corporations in just six months alone, with nearly every major Silicon Valley venture-capital firm investing in certified B Corporations. These are businesses that balance purpose and profit and are legally required to consider the impact of their decisions on their workers, customers, suppliers, community and the environment. Year-on-year data from 2018 also shows that UK B Corps grew at a rate of 14% compared to the country's GDP growth rate of 0.5%, suggesting that customers are actively choosing to spend more money with ethical businesses, while employers are achieving

Wallace and Gromit

higher results within these companies.

Meanwhile, in the kids' media business, the UK's Aardman, responsible for *Wallace & Gromit* and *Shaun the Sheep*, made the headlines after handing over a 75% stake in the business to their 140 employees. While the deal assures the company's independence and helps avoid the usual route of growing its value for a potential sale (a common practice that solely benefits shareholders and leaves employees on the side lines) - this strategy also brings the entire team to the forefront of the business, retaining and attracting talent and encouraging and rewarding productivity.

Shaun the Sheep

When it comes to family and children's content, high-quality entertainment will always be the leading criteria for consumption, but new ingredients are now being added to the mix. In

2019, research produced by The Shift Project, named *Climate Crisis: The Unsustainable Use of Online Video*, revealed alarming data about the hidden environmental impact of online video consumption. It was found that the yearly greenhouse gas emissions of combined VoD services are equivalent to those produced by a country the size of Chile. Up until now, the size of libraries and price points have been the main weapons in the streaming war. But finding more eco-friendly solutions to limit emissions could deliver a significant competitive advantage, especially given consumers' willingness to switch brands to those which are purpose-driven.

Elsewhere, toy companies need to recognise and respond to a fast-rising movement against plastics that is shaping consumer behaviour. With 40% of Millennials and Generation Z consumers reporting that a business goal should be to improve society, it makes sense for the toy industry to recognise the investment in eco-toys and the eradication of plastic as their first priorities. While giants such as Hasbro, Mattel and LEGO have been either too slow or too restrained in their initiatives, newcomers like BioBuddi, a European eco-friendly toy company that uses materials made from sugar cane waste in the manufacture of its product range, are showing that 100% plastic- free toys are already a reality.

It is undeniable that this new decade holds more challenges than solutions - especially as the world contends with the COVID-19 pandemic - but an entrepreneur is disruptive by nature. A desire to start a business comes from seeing a better way of doing something or identifying something new that needs doing.

With this in mind, I can only hope that the search for purpose will disrupt our industry, while also inspiring growth within the premise of serving the common good and finding new creative solutions for a more egalitarian society and ecological balance. After all, the kids' entertainment industry should have children's wellbeing at its heart and working to ensure a liveable future for them should inform all our business decisions.

annie-spratt-unsplash

THE OFFICE

Rapidly changing media landscapes can mean trouble ahead for providers of Children's Media. It's not all about giving the audience what they want. There are challenges at every turn. How do we regulate the digital space to protect the audience from online abuse and inappropriate material? What role does media play in their lives – is it just for entertainment or are they using it as a tool for other means? Home schooling saw the rise of lessons online for many children, and saw the BBC step effortlessly into a role they've been doing for years. It provides the BBC with a strong argument for survival, but it's part of a wider question about the role of Public Service Broadcasting and by extension the future of the BBC.

THE OFFICE

RADICAL THINKING:
Can A New Public Service Broadcast Concept Reshape The Children's Media Landscape?

COLIN WARD
Deputy Director, The Children's Media Foundation

It's a given that we all support the idea of a thriving, UK children's production community, drawing on storytelling traditions unique to this country. It makes perfect commercial sense; in a crowded global market, you need content that stands out from the crowd. If all we were doing was imitating what other producers are creating around the world then the future would look very bleak indeed. Why would platforms commission an imitation when they can get the original?

The UK's production community's USP is the rich, diverse cultural heritage that we all absorb when we walk out of our front doors. Those are the inspirational experiences they add into the mix to help create exciting new content. But, as we all know, when you've got a great story you want to share with the audience, you still need to find a commissioner with the money to pay for that content. And that journey has become progressively more challenging as children's media has become a genuinely global industry. In fact, it's getting so hard that a government not known for its love of market interventions has set up the Young Audiences Content Fund to encourage commissioners to support UK-originated content.

The YAC Fund is a pilot project run by the British Film Institute, and the government will use the information gleaned  to further develop its thinking around a specific question; how can we create a UK children's media production landscape that embraces the very best of the global market and also protects and grows the unique, home-grown talent that is the future of our industry?

The Children's Media Foundation has decided to seize this small window of opportunity to influence government thinking and is asking some fundamental questions about the future of children's media in the UK. We can see the BBC coming under increasing pressure and there is not much sign of the commercial PSB's regaining their appetite for increasing their spending to make significantly more high quality, UK-originated content. And of course, without competition for content, the BBC is weaker. Perhaps now is the time to redefine what we understand by the term 'public service broadcasting'? Should we focus instead on the concept of 'public service content'? Does it matter where children find new content that reflects their own lives, as long as they can find it somewhere?

This is not about blowing the cobwebs off old ideas. No one wants to turn the clock back to some mythical golden era and although this is definitely a worthwhile project, it is not 'worthy'; it is a commercially-driven initiative. We need to restate the core values of public service broadcasting for children in terms that reflect the current situation and are fit for a 21st century industry. We need to help government develop a framework of ideas that will help them engage with the widest possible range of producers and platforms, because that is how the UK production community will survive and prosper.

And, arguably, there are wider considerations for the economy. A failure to produce culturally-relevant media content for our children must surely impact on the ideas of future creators working in the UK's media industries. How can we expect the next generation of directors, producers and writers to create uniquely British stories if their media experiences as children do nothing to nurture their identity and unique sense of self?

The Children's Media Foundation does not have the answers to these difficult questions, which is why we are launching an inquiry into the future of public service content for children in an effort to find those answers. Over the next nine months, we will be consulting as widely as possible with everyone involved in, and concerned about, the creation of children's media content in the UK. That includes producers and broadcasters, but also parents and children, writers, directors, children's charities and academic and commercial researchers.

Over the years there have been many inquiries into public service content, but this will be the first to focus solely on children and the media they consume and need. We will examine our shared concepts of public service content and discuss how we can adapt those concepts to operate effectively in a media industry dominated by global streaming services. We will start from first principles with no presuppositions, other than the importance of putting the needs of the audience at the heart of our work.

This is an opportunity to influence the government's thinking. Our objective is to agree a set of practical steps to maintain the strengths of the UK's production community, build new relationships within the sector and to propose a set of metrics to ensure the continuation and growth of public service content in the 21st century broadcasting landscape.

If you would like to be involved, please get in touch at either of the email addresses below. Thanks.

director@thechildrensmediafoundation.org
research@thechildrensmediafoundation.org

THE OFFICE

BBC BITESIZE DAILY AND LOCKDOWN

HELEN FOULKES
Head of BBC Education

In March 2020, the UK went into lockdown, schools across the country closed their doors to pupils except for children of key workers and vulnerable children. Parents forced to work from home were given the task of educating their children.

As BBC Education, our role is to create guides, lessons and support for students aged 4-16 on *BBC Bitesize*; free resources for teachers on *BBC Teach*; and to listen to the issues affecting children and parents and develop these into impactful campaigns. At this point, one of the biggest issues affecting children was that they were unable to go to school and parents and teachers were looking to the BBC for support. As a result, we launched a new education service called BBC Bitesize Daily.

Bitesize Daily launched on April 20th 2020, just five weeks after schools closed, and was the biggest education effort that the BBC has ever undertaken. We worked with teachers, schools and parents to make sure children had the support they needed to keep learning.

We provided 14 weeks of educational programmes and lessons: nearly 300 lessons on TV and Red Button; 2000 online lessons; and extra support to help children, parents and teachers. We made sure that every child in the UK had access to content that was relevant to their nation's curriculum.

On BBC *Bitesize Daily Online*, we delivered three new curriculum led lessons every day for years 1-10 covering the core subjects of maths, english and science, alongside history, geography, religious studies, music, computer science, welsh and design and technology. While on the iPlayer and Red Button, Bitesize Daily broadcast 297 programmes for primary and secondary students covering a wide range of subjects.

But we couldn't have done this on our own, this was a huge collaborative effort. Internally, within the BBC, we worked with iPlayer, radio and online services. Every week, BBC Sounds delivered two podcasts aimed at parents: *Bitesize Primary Survival Podcast* and *Bitesize Secondary Survival Podcast*, giving advice to parents as they navigated home-schooling. On BBC Four, documentaries in the arts and history were shown aimed at older students.

We also worked closely with educational consultants and teachers to shape lesson content, some even appeared on screen. And we worked with over 100 partners including Premier League, Royal Shakespeare Company and Science Museum Group who all supported Bitesize Daily, providing a wealth of content for the BBC to use within lessons. In the first two weeks 100 partners shared over 300 activities with us. And top BBC talent including Sir David Attenborough, Jodie Whittaker and Jesse Lingard were only too happy to get involved.

One of the key things we set out to achieve with Bitesize Daily was to make the content accessible to everyone and I think that is the main reason why Bitesize Daily has been so popular. It also allowed people to use as much or as little as they needed. It was important to provide content on different platforms – programmes on BBC iPlayer and a variety of content online – so that people can access whatever works best for them. I think parents and teachers also appreciated the fact that we delivered content throughout the whole of the summer term. Of course, we would never try to take the place of schools or teachers in the classroom, but in the time of a national pandemic, Bitesize Daily has been a phenomenal resource for parent and teachers and we have been inundated with feedback telling us how useful our content has been.

In those 14 weeks, record numbers of people came to Bitesize Daily. There have been over 6 million BBC iPlayer requests for Bitesize Daily TV programmes; the BBC Bitesize Daily online lessons had almost 4 million views every week; and we have received countless emails and social media posts praising or content.

It took a huge collaborative effort across the Childrens and Education department to produce Bitesize Daily and we were fortunate that we were able to work with talented staff whose productions had been put on hold due to the pandemic on our broadcast output. At its peak, we had around 130 people working on Bitesize Daily and many of them, particularly on the online side were working at home – in their bedrooms, in spare rooms and around kitchen tables. I am so proud of how everyone worked together to create something on this scale in such a short space of time.

There have been so many highlights across the 14 weeks but I wanted to share with you some of my personal favourite moments which include:

Sir David Attenborough delivering Science

THE OFFICE

and Geography lessons for Primary children. He enjoyed doing it so much that he worked with us to create an additional Summer Challenge for children asking them to create their own nature diary.

Singer Liam Payne sharing the meaning behind his lyrics in The Big Song, part of Bitesize Daily's Creativity Week for Secondary children.

I loved seeing so many big names get on board to read stories to children as part of *The Book Club*. David Walliams, Stephen Fry and Jesse Lingard, to name just a few.

And who didn't enjoy learning Spanish with Manchester City striker Sergio Aguero?! He delivered some engaging language lessons for KS3 students which proved to be really popular whether you are a red or a blue!

Obviously we're hoping that all schools will be fully open again in September for all students but our commitment to the nation's children continues. We will be providing an online catch-up service for primary children focusing on the key concepts of Maths and English that children might have missed last year. And we will also have learning resources available for all children which can be used in school or at home and will help children make a success of the autumn curriculum.

BBC Education's vision has always been to transform lives through education. By responding quickly to a nationwide crisis, I hope we've shown that we can adapt our content and resources to support children, and their parents and teachers, whatever and wherever, they are learning.

TIDINGS OF CONTENT AND JOY
The Progress of the Young Audiences Content Fund

JACKIE EDWARDS
Head of BFI Young Audience Content Fund

Last year, in this very book, I described the Young Audiences Content Fund administered by the BFI as a reason to be cheerful. In 2020, the year of living virtually, we need all the cheer we can get our (clean) hands on.

Back in May, I was talking to Simone Tennant from the TV Collective. I'd just had a Covid test, and due to some imprudent swabbing, like a pony with laryngitis - I was a little hoarse, and frankly a little down. Simone, a wise woman, was talking about her coping strategy for lockdown – "**you have to find some joy in every day**". Very wise. Shortly after, the first draft of our year one evaluation report plopped into my inbox, confirming that our first year of supporting development and production of brilliant new content for this country's young people, was

THE OFFICE

broadly delivering on intentions as well as guiding future efforts for improvement. Joy.

When we launched the Fund in April 2019, I talked about it being a community endeavour – producers needed to bring their best ideas, broadcasters needed to reach further down the side of the sofa to commission the new, the big and the brave, and that we all need to support new voices, to tell representative and authentic stories from a wider range of communities. The ambition of the fund is to create shows that really reflect the lives of our young people in all ways. They say it takes a village to raise a child: well, as the first year has shown, it's taken a production and broadcast community to make this Fund work. Only one year on, we have had 227 applications and made 81 awards to support

the development and production of brilliant new content.

The Fund is certainly helping address the programme deficits described by Ofcom in 2018, but in more ways than we could have hoped for. Authentic stories, representing diverse communities from all of the UK, displaying the best wit, wisdom and stellar creativity that this community has to offer. Best ideas have been brought forward; mature companies are nurturing new voices; new voices and new companies are taking the plunge themselves and bringing the fantastic! Great shows are being commissioned by engaged and excited broadcasters, and the power of a modest, but well-structured development process – focussing thought, upskilling talent,

and outputting high quality commission-ready ideas – is something very much noted by broadcasters already.

Together we are revivifying what was a tired and impoverished landscape.

So far so good, but this information was mostly collected from times when we could roam free and lead unrestricted lives. What now?

The impact of lockdown and restricted living is becoming clearer every day, and the profound impact on business, the economy, our health is being realised. A generation of children with their education, friendships and lives interrupted. You have to look hard to find the joy sometimes, but look we must. For the now and for the future.

Fund HQ activity was uninterrupted by lockdown, and continues to provide much needed support for development and for new and ongoing productions. The Fund continuity was and is a positive. But more positive was the reminder, if any were needed, of the huge importance of free-to-access, regulated, public service broadcast. It informed, it educated, it entertained and it engaged young minds, helping them deal with this unprecedented public health crisis. It showed us all who we are and how to be in the worst of times.

We adapted our Fund communications plan to embrace public service broadcast and all who care about it with our See Yourself on Screen campaign. Led by wonderful Dr Ranj from the CBeebies' show *Get Well Soon*, we threw a creative challenge to young audiences, asking them to pitch a TV show they would like to see and that described their lockdown life.

This became a properly joyful community

activity that saw public service broadcasters, The Children's Media

 Conference, PACT, Animation UK, Into Film, BAFTA and Northern Ireland Screen join hands to support this initiative to reach out to our youngest audiences. 15 winning pitches were selected by dedicated teams of judges from these organisations, the winners were coached and mentored by top telly talent like Jessica Hynes, Reggie Yates, Konnie Huq, Robert Popper and Rob Delaney, and the resultant films were  broadcast, 3 each on Milkshake, E4, CITV, TG4 and S4C. Joy.

With public service broadcast facing uncertain times we'll need to join hands again soon undoubtedly. The biggest and best argument for public service broadcast is always and ever, brilliant content. Programmes that talk about us and speak directly to us. Now more than ever, our young people need public service content that informs, educates and entertains, that affirms, that reflects, that reassures and most importantly gives them joy. The Fund is here to help you deliver that joy.

www.bfi.org.uk/supporting-uk-film/production-development-funding/young-audiences-content-fund

(The Young Audiences Content Fund is a UK Government supported initiative administered by the BFI)

THE GENERATION GAME
Can The BBC Win Over Today's Young Audience

EDITED BY MICHAEL WILSON AND NEIL FOWLER

The Future of the BBC is one that Children's Media Foundation has been discussing for a while, as the importance of PSB and the question of who will fund that service is an issue of great concern to CMF and the Children's Media industry as a major provider of PSB to young audiences. As yet, an answer is elusive.

This year saw the publication of an insightful book called The Generation Game. The editors sought opinions from industry experts on the future of the BBC. The question for them, however, was not should the BBC survive, but can the BBC survive.

We have chosen four articles from that book that highlight the challenges the BBC faces in today's multi platform digital and streaming culture. They offer thoughts and potential solutions. The editors and authors have given us permission to reproduce their articles in the CMF Yearbook 2020 and they provide a different perspective on the question of the BBC's future. They also add important and relevant voices to the discussion.

CHILDREN'S MEDIA YEARBOOK 2020

OK, BOOMERS! HERE ARE OUR CHALLENGES AND OPPORTUNITIES

VICTORIA MCCOLLUM

Why do millennials and younger merely tolerate such a potentially loveable broadcaster as the BBC? Victoria McCollum, who works with this 'lost generation', outlines five reasons why the corporation, despite its admirable efforts, is struggling to engage them

It will make for uncomfortable but necessary reading for the BBC, but worth it. This chapter has insights drawn from my own experience and from group discussions with more than 150 BSc Cinematic Arts students enrolled on my Business of Film and TV module at Ulster University. Prepare yourselves....

1. We are broke and miserable: Lose the licence fee

CHALLENGE: There's a reason why the American-animated sitcom, *Top Cat*, about a hustling homeless chancer, is being used to advertise mortgages for the Halifax. TC, who lives in a back-alley dustbin, and who I engaged with every morning before school as a child, shares our cash-strapped plight. World-weary millennials have ditched television licences for dystopian binges on Netflix. Why? Because, we're saddled with debt, unable to accumulate wealth, and (mostly) stuck in low-benefit, dead-end jobs.

Millennials and younger will never gain the financial security and living standards that our parents (Baby Boomers and Gen X-ers) enjoyed. The year is 2020, a peak earning year according to Business Insider, and we find ourselves, once again, marching toward meltdown as we enter an economic cataclysm more severe than the Great Recession. We, the millennials and younger, will be the first generations in modern British history to end up poorer than our parents. We are vulnerable. We are heavily dependent on the gig economy.

Paying a hefty licence fee feels like death by a thousand cuts. Believe me, I know. I once worked as a Complaints Advisor for BBC Audience Services. The truth is, we deeply desire access to the 16 episodes of *Blue Planet* on iPlayer, which is astonishing to watch, but the 28 of +2000 episodes of *Bargain Hunt* available is a deal breaker for us. For millennials and younger, the licence fee is equivalent to one coffee every week for an entire year. That's equivalent to 24 months of Netflix!

OPPORTUNITY: Adopt a Prime video-style subscription model, in place of the licence fee, or lose a generation.

85

THE GENERATION GAME

2. We surf whilst we watch: Meet us where we are

CHALLENGE: It feels as if the BBC, despite its efforts, takes a tone-deaf approach to contemporary digital culture. Just as we, the millennials and younger, are required to build a strong online presence in order to engage potential employers, so should the BBC construct a more innovative online persona, integrating popular internet phenomena, to prove worthy of our wallets.

The ways in which the BBC currently engages social media platforms are far from under-30s friendly. For example, my students greatly prefer Vice news' Twitter account (@ViceNews) to the BBC's (@BBCNews), because it feels more like an edgy digital outsider than the slick global empire that it is.

The BBC's official Instagram channel (@BBC) does feature some memes, which is a start, considering millennials and younger use these bottom-up expressions to entertain, inform and educate each other on a daily basis. Memes shape public conversation.

What is most surprising is that the BBC has virtually no presence on the most popular short-form video-sharing apps with cult-followings, like Tik Tok. Early-career female journalists, like Sophia Smith Galer and Emma Bentley, often share unofficial video content on Tik Tok about working at the BBC, which regularly goes viral.

However, one can only assume that the efforts of both journalists, who have now accrued more than 12,000 followers, are being ignored by those in the upper echelons of senior management at the BBC, who are, granted, not likely on Tik Tok.

That said, the broadcaster should be sincerely commended for its latest efforts to engage millennials and younger. Recent BBC news podcast The Next Episode genuinely engages with stories that matter to us, as does BBC Three's *Normal People* about love, sex, and class in contemporary Ireland, and new digital video platform BBC Reel, which features factual shorts about gender, race, fitness, addiction, psychology and sex. If only this relatable content was not forcibly squeezed through such traditional channels, which often feel stale in style and function to millennials and younger. The dog has mastered the tricks, but its appearance is of consequence too.

OPPORTUNITY: Tell comprehensive stories through multiple reinforcing channels. Invest in original, personal and authentic social content. Bring a strategic and creative approach to social media. We do not expect excessive hashtags, emojis, or phrases like 'it's lit', but we do expect to be retweeted and engaged by questions, polls, sassy replies and irreverent comments. Embrace your place in popular culture. There's a reason why no one wants to 'BBC and chill'. Meet us where we are or lose a generation.

3. We have trust issues: Reinvent quality news

CHALLENGE: Millennials and younger, whilst we adore radio because it feels like a present-tense authentic medium in which events unfold right before our ears, don't trust traditional media and advertising. We are forced to consume it, but its tactics so often comes across as pushy and disingenuous. We look to our network for recommendations – to influencers. We look for social proof in an era saturated with choice. For example, I recently watched Netflix's *Tiger King* due to the recommendation of the masses on my Twitter feed, which tends to feature film and TV academics, critics and friends. 'Fomo' brought me to *Tiger King* – the fear of missing out.

Tiger King

We trust user-generated, personalised content, such as tweets, to a much greater degree than we trust branded content. Video is the differentiator for us – the great empathy machine. We dig decelerated headlines, which expand, via video, into opportunities for us to deeply connect with people and cultures. Speed-read headlines, such as '70 killed in suspected chemical attack in Douma', cause us to recoil and disengage.

The BBC's fiercest rivals, such as *Vice News* and *BuzzFeed*, immerse us in the action, using innovative journalistic storytelling strategies to build deep empathetic connections with their audiences. Vice News journalists go there, they experience it, they talk about what they see – and they look just like us, as opposed to white, middle-aged men, which fortunately appear to constitute an endangered species on digital media.

Millennials and younger also have powerful bullshit detectors. We know when we're being sold a piece of commoditised information, which is a slave to editorial guidelines, over a sincere opinion or perspective. We want to know what people think. We dig multi-perspectivity. Storytelling is important to us. We want to hear original stories – sociologically-relevant conversation-starters – not so dictated to by broadcast rules or advertisers.

Millennials and younger want to consume editorial that involves a deep integration of tech, from genuinely pro-digital culture news outlets that do not feel particularly nostalgic about the good old (legacy news) days.

OPPORTUNITY: The BBC has been active in the digital field for 26 years now; it has learned about how this space functions, and is attuned to the pace of the industry and how innovation is best approached. Engage, via immersive journalism, with the issues that traditional outlets are known not to engage with, such as antifascist youth movements, student protests, cutting-edge new art forms, cannabis, new-age health, the world's oppressed, and LGBT culture. Anchor and steer your news with young and relatable on-air correspondents who appear to take on the establishment or lose a generation.

4. We cultivate a culture of inclusion: Concentrate on reach not ratings

CHALLENGE: Millennials and younger are more connected to global citizenship and human rights than nationalism. We are morally minded and ethically informed global citizens that enjoy genre-defining and boundary-pushing content.

For us, the BBC so often seems to care more about ratings than it does reach. Millennials and younger know only too well that minority ethnic groups, LBGT people and those with disabilities make up a shameful percentage of the BBC's creative workforce and we assume this discrepancy bleeds into programming.

THE GENERATION GAME

When in search of British content, my students often turn to Channel 4 for an authentic portrayal of their lives, claiming that the BBC fails to connect with their spine – "it feels white, middle class, mostly concerned with the South East."

On the other hand, we know that the BBC's competitors target programming at specific demographics using viewership data. Believe me, I was working at HBO in NYC when it launched its on-demand streaming service HBO Go, which was the result of micro-profiling, micro-targeting and micro-aggregation on a global scale – something in which Netflix and Amazon Prime also have unique expertise.

Where is the BBC's insatiable appetite for data-gathering, which would help the broadcaster to ring-fence funds for diverse programming? Recently, and in reference to audience data and algorithms, Charlotte Moore when BBC Director of Content stated, "I don't believe any amount of data can tell you what to commission next."

Why on earth not? Is it not one of the BBC's core public purposes to reflect and serve the UK's diverse communities? Perhaps, data-led decision making would allow the BBC to recognise that its audience is increasingly diverse. After all, why would a viewer want to watch programmes that consistently fail to resonate with any of their personal experiences?

OPPORTUNITY: The BBC should focus on the reach of specific programmes over audience size. True inclusion does not start and end, for example, with token casting. 'Progressive' re-imaginings of shows like *Doctor Who*, for instance, are emblematic of the problem: attempting to rewrite the past, instead of looking to the future.

Diversity is not a varnish you can apply to old familiar stories. Millennials and younger crave an expanded universe. Take responsibility for ensuring improved balance through in-house measuring of progress on equality and internal reflection on that progress. Integrate cultural diversity, inclusion and equity into all aspects of your operations or lose a generation.

5. Quality TV is important to us: Make more TV that no longer resembles TV

CHALLENGE: Millennials and younger look for experiences over possessions. We are lured in by networks with strong legitimisation strategies, such as "It's not TV, it's HBO", which ultimately promise a high-quality viewing experience.

For us, quality TV is best defined by what it is not 'regular television'. In fact, the less television resembles television – the more we like it. Netflix is well aware of this. There is a reason why the term 'Original' is front and centre of its own promotional discourses. We want novelty, originality, prestige – new storytelling practices unimaginable in the past.

Give us television that appeals to us technologically and aesthetically and we will binge, and feast on it. Millennials and younger rate Toms over Nike because we believe that the brand's purpose is to create world value, not just shareholder value.

In other words, its purpose aligns with what's important to us. The BBC has a well-established reputation for culturally valuable programming. Millennials and younger see this expressed most explicitly in the content of BBC Four. Why? Because it feels as if the depth and substance of content on the channel is made to appeal to a much narrower audience with specific tastes, than, say, the content of BBC Two, which is much too broad to interest us.

Millennials and younger are used to being classified and identified as an audience through the use of narrow frameworks. Sharpened storytelling is the new black. We adore programming that creatively engages with genre material, leans toward the controversial and realistic, experiments with narrative complexity and breaks the established rules of television.

Give us something to think about. Give us sharp social and cultural criticism. I have had more water-cooler conversations with my students about *Fleabag* (BBC Three), *Gentleman Jack* (BBC One), *Killing Eve* (BBC One) and *Twin* (BBC Four) in the last year than I have had about any other programmes.

OPPORTUNITY: Invest in a narrow range of expensive, high-end distinctively British stories that millennials and younger can anticipate before broadcast and savour afterward. Instead of seeking to educate, inform and entertain us, enlighten, challenge and involve us – and gain a generation. We deeply want to belong to a broadcaster that deeply wants us to belong.

About the writer

Dr Victoria McCollum is an award-wining lecturer in Cinematic Arts at Ulster University, Northern Ireland, and has previously held positions at BBC, ITV, MTV and HBO. She has published several cutting-edge books on film, media and television, such as HBO's Original Voices: Race, Gender, Sexuality and Power (2018); Make America Hate Again: Trump-Era Horror and the Politics of Fear (2019); and Resist: Protest and Resistance Media in Trump-Era USA (2020). Victoria believes in engaging students as partners and is dedicated to creating transformative learning opportunities for her students encouraging them to develop their own identities as filmmakers, producers and content creators. You can find her on Twitter: @Vic_McC.

THE GENERATION GAME

GEN Z – PUBLIC SERVICE TV'S LOST GENERATION

CLAIRE HUNGATE

Technology has granted the audience unprecedented control over and access to the content it views. This has caused a huge change in who creates content, how that content is produced, how stories are told and the way they are consumed. The biggest impact has been to those born after 2001 – the so-called Generation Z; and as the next consumer generation they are critical to the future economics of the media landscape. We are bombarded with statistics telling us that linear TV has lost that audience. Claire Hungate asks why is that loss so stark and whether linear can win them back?

My twins are four years old and until (very) recently they thought the television set was called CBeebies; now that's what I call brand (dis-) attribution. So how is it that the BBC can entirely lose that audience when they are old enough to discover Superheroes and Disney – and not win them back until they are 50+?

What has caused the seismic movements to the broadcast landscape over the last number of years and how did the BBC (and UK linear broadcasters generally) miss the memo?

Is it technology, or is it content – is content still king or has distribution taken the crown? And has linear TV's denial of the power of audience been its downfall?

I spent 18 years in TV production; helping grow 'super indie' Shed Media and then selling it to Warner Bros, then an entrepreneurial studio grown from creativity – now Warner Media, owned by a telecoms company. The global media market and the economics that drive it have been changing rapidly; the highly leveraged titans of global media, such as Apple, Comcast, Disney, AT&T, Netflix and the not-so-highly-leveraged Amazon will battle it out to be the winner of the eyeballs. The UK domestic public service broadcast (PSB) market has limped to keep pace with this change.

In 2017 I transitioned into the world of digital – of social media and social video content – and it became obvious that the driving force in the evolution of content wasn't broadcasters – it was the audience.

Social media studios understand audience because their lives revolve around them; audience is everything – audience engagement, interaction, appreciation – you can see it all in real time; it looms large. And it is what motivates everything you do; every post, every piece of content, every comment, when you post, what you post, if you post. If something doesn't drive audience engagement – you take it down – immediately. But it's about watching audience reaction in real time and reacting to that audience reaction.

In this regard particularly, I think 'old media' can learn a lot from the new.
A new in which audiences congregate around passion points, both passionate niches (think Esports) and global consumer brands (think *Friends*); a new in which audiences want to be part of a community which social media allows, a new in which an ability to tap into culture in an authentic way, can garner real brand loyalty. Netflix gets this…it seeks to make niches global, super serving audiences content to build viewer engagement, stickiness and brand attribution.

Sadly, for me, as someone who has spent most of my career in content production, I actually think it's technology, rather than content, that is the great enabler amid all this movement – the conduit to giving the audience the expectation of content, anywhere, always, on demand. Content comes a close second; great content can still cut through but it requires equally great distribution and accessibility to do so. And where Netflix has the commercial freedom and audacity to experiment with content and distribution, the UK PSBs have not.

Technology and its evolution have shaped a generation and that generation is now the emergent consumer group driving the media economy.

What is Generation Z?

According to Bloomberg, using United Nations data, almost a third of the world's population is Generation Z –that is – born around 2001 or later:

- that's the year Al Qaeda launched an attack on the Twin Towers;
- the year the first *Harry Potter*, *Lord of the Rings* and *Shrek* films were released and Britney and Justin donned their iconic coordinating denim outfits for the American Music Awards;
- and in technology: Wikipedia went on-line and the first iPod was released.

A year later wireless headphones hit the streets, followed by camera phones and smart phones; YouTube in 2005; Apple TV in 2007; Hulu in 2008; and by the time Gen Z was ten it could watch content on an iPad or a smart TV –the perfect groundwork laid for it to stream Netflix in 2010.

Gen Z is coming of age and now comprises 20 per cent of the global workforce; its members can vote and are dominating the consumer landscape.

How can broadcasters and content producers engage, entertain and market to a generation born with smart phones in its hands, which has an intuitive connection to technology, which is used to consuming content and stories in an entirely different way than we are used to distributing or telling them – a generation which doesn't remember a world without Netflix, Amazon, Apple, YouTube and Facebook or smart TVs and phones. A generation which demands choice, value for money, great technology and content everywhere, whenever it wants it.

So, what do we know about this Generation Z, described below by a 2019 Snapchat report:

"They're the hyper-connected, highly opinionated generation, moved to activism as the internet and social media landscape has made them acutely conscious of and concerned about world events. Having lived in an era of overall progress when it comes to issues like marriage equality and body positivity, they're forging new territory in broader conversations about identity; this is the cohort of gender fluidity, diversity and inclusivity in all its forms."

Its members are digital natives and content consumption is a lifestyle for them.

- They are technology reliant.
- They are multi taskers and could be using up to five screens at once.
- They were born during a time of heightened global tension with terrorism and Al-Qaeda dominating the news, making them anxious about safety; the Covid-19 pandemic has only furthered this anxiety.
- They were born during recession, which makes them pragmatic about money; this will potentially be exacerbated in the current climate.
- They don't see difference or talk about diversity – they live with it.
- They are health conscious – less likely to smoke or drink – and are happy to socialise online without going to parties.
- But they value their privacy and are aware of data issues online.
- Professionally, they are entrepreneurial and worried about their future and will often have more than one job (the so called 'gig economy').

Smartphone use is pretty much ubiquitous in this generation and about half of them are connected online about ten hours a day. Media consumption for Gen Z is embedded in their daily lives so they are not even consciously making a decision to consume content. Among teens – 13-18-year-olds – smartphones are used almost three hours a day to consume TV shows, videos, music, games and social media.

As for content the good news is that Gen Z love it. They want as much as they can possibly get – be that creator content on YouTube or Tik Tok or 236 episodes of 20-year-old sitcom Friends. The bad news for linear broadcast networks is that they are tied neither to TV services to watch it nor to a big piece of kit in the living room.

Gen Z tend to use over-the-top services that are not tied to TV services. They do watch TV, but are more likely to consume content on Netflix and YouTube.

According to 59 per cent of Gen Z video consumption is done via over-the-top (OTT) services vs 29 per cent for TV; 70 per cent of Gen Z watch more than two hours of YouTube each day, as opposed to their predecessors – the Millennials – for whom TV and cable are used together with OTT services for media consumption.

The drivers for consumption by Gen Z are increasingly shifting as they spend more time on their smart phones engaged in social media apps. For Gen Z, social media is a major way of engaging with a community, as opposed to being just a digital broadcasting platform. It's also a way to participate – to be part of the conversation; hence the domination of gaming and Esports via sites like Twitch and YouTube.

Netflix invested in Generation Z

And as regards their consumption of media, content is a lifestyle, not just entertainment. It's not their attention spans that are short – it's their interest span; their bullshit detector is highly developed and they can easily sniff out content produced by those who aren't genuinely tapped into their culture or that doesn't feel authentic. Getting traditional TV producers to produce content for digital platforms for a Gen Z audience simply does not cut it – the way stories are told and consumed – the beats of a story – are different.

For those seeking to attract that audience; they should think about engaging communities around passion points, niches or big consumer brands that they care about – if it disappears from their feed or your service tomorrow – will they notice and if they do – will they care? Even Netflix look for niches and passions to attract audience behind their big tent pole shows. This isn't just about an amorphous age group; within that are 'taste groups' – communities – passion lead niches.

Another interesting contrast between Netflix and the BBC is that, while the BBC was closing BBC Three as a linear channel and halving its budget, Netflix realised that generally, investment in premium content for the under 30s was sparse. Not only did it invest in this demographic – it actively wooed them with marketing campaigns directed at them and by advertising across the platforms they love, in a manner that engaged and appealed. In the UK certainly, a generation on which the BBC turned its back and withheld their allowance, found a new home – with Netflix, the parents who loved and spoiled them.

Influencers who make their name on social media platforms like Instagram, Tik Tok, and YouTube are increasingly important drivers of consumption and content itself is adapting accordingly. Whether it's music or video, influencer content is short-form, off-the-cuff, authentic, shareable and highly relatable. This makes it easy for Gen Z fans to consume the content fluidly across multiple channels and devices throughout the day.

Influencers have a strong presence and built-in distribution, but they also have a deeply personal relationship with their fans, which allows them to create storylines they already know will resonate with their audience – they live and die with their audience.

This is a generation which is audience first, digital first, social first, video first. Content is consumed in a seamless and organic way. Businesses in the media and entertainment ecosystem that adapt accordingly will win. Gen Zs are watching TV content and are following TV brands – they just aren't necessarily watching

THE GENERATION GAME

them on scheduled linear TV.

As an industry it was TV's failure to keep track of audiences and effectively communicate with them on their terms and on their preferred digital platforms, that means the PSB broadcasters are so woefully behind the digital disruption that their frenemies at YouTube and Facebook have wreaked since Gen Z entered the world.

And now Tik Tok, a platform with an almost 70 per cent under 30 demographic and which allows everyone to be an influencer and for their post to effectively reach a large audience (almost impossible now for a new entrant to YouTube for example) is stealing a march on the competition.

Today, six years after moving BBC Three online and slashing its budget, the BBC has re-upped Three's content spend and is talking about moving it back on the box. But why? Isn't that too little too late – isn't that just tokenism?

It might give a bigger platform to content produced for BBC Three – and yes, it's true there has been some cut-through content – but will it bring a new Gen Z audience to linear TV or to the BBC's other channels? Will it be powerful enough to make Gen Z care about the BBC in the same way Baby Boomers care about the BBC? Or would the BBC be better off investing in the content, the marketing and distribution of that content and rethinking the branding around BBC Three?

Would it be better off fighting regulatory, commercial restrictions and attribution issues that prevent it from taking its content and its dialogue with its desired audiences to the platforms where they play; new audiences who will engage with, participate in and care about the future of the BBC – where they can build loyalty and re-engage the attribution instinct that was so strong at the age of four?

In order to survive in a licence fee- (even partially) funded environment, the BBC must harness the power of Generation Z, and Generation Alpha that follows it. We must question whether investing in a new linear TV channel right now is the most effective method of doing that in a world where resources are stretched, consumer choice is huge and only increasing day by day, and the well-funded competition just keeps getting stronger.

About the writer

Claire Hungate is an internationally recognised expert in the media space; her experience spans the financing, production, distribution and commercialisation of audio-visual content across multiple distribution platforms. She has spent the last 20 years in executive roles in the television and digital media sectors, including running some of the biggest and most successful TV production companies in the world including Wall to Wall, Shed Media and Warner Bros. TV UK. .

Claire is a board member at Media Capital Technologies, a global entertainment company which funds premium content; advisor to the board at Chimp Productions, Richard Hammond's (Grand Tour, Top Gear) content production company and chair of, and an investor in, The Nerve Media Group, an online music library aimed at the TV production sector. In 2019 she was chair of the content steering committee of the International Broadcasting Conference and is a well-respected speaker on the international conference circuit.

Twitter @ClaireHungate
https://www.linkedin.com/in/clairehungate/.

A TIKTOK-ING CLOCK HEADING TOWARDS REGENERATION – OR NOT?

COLIN MANN

How do young people consume content? Does the manner in which they do provide any clues to how they might engage with the BBC in the future? Colin Mann finds out first hand from a group of teenagers on their thoughts on the corporation and whether these insights offer any hope. It might be an uphill struggle.

In seeking to address the issues raised in this book, I found myself at an early disadvantage: no close family who could be categorised as the 'missing generation', and under lockdown, no easy prospect of gauging their thoughts on the matter. However, a close associate with children falling into that demographic, and whose kids' school and college friends were keen to contribute, undertook to host an online discussion.

At the outset, one participant admitted that they hadn't watched the BBC since actor Matt Smith "stopped being *Doctor Who*", around 2014, when he was replaced by the older Peter Capaldi. This group, although far from what might be considered an empirical sample, proved very opinionated and passionate about the topic, particularly in terms of their current perception of the corporation and its funding model.

"The BBC is irrelevant to our generation," declared one. "You don't get taxed for watching things online," added another. All participants saw the licence fee as a tax, with the potential penalties for non-payment a cause for concern. "If you don't pay, you go to jail," observed one. "It's like 1984."

"The more they try to force us to pay, the less we want to watch," warned another.

What one participant described as 'bundling' was not favoured. "I only want to watch *Killing Eve*, not the rest. Why should I pay if I don't want to watch all of it?" "Forcing people to pay is where it's going wrong," said another, with others agreeing that they would be happy to pay to watch it on another platform.

Killing Eve

THE GENERATION GAME

"The BBC should concentrate on making programmes and sell to the Netflixes," was one suggestion. "You can engage with that platform and will pay for that content." "We know the BBC has got to make money somehow, we know that's how it is, but we just don't agree with how they are doing it," summed up one contributor. There certainly wasn't a sense that this group wanted 'something for nothing'.

A question of image

The perception of the licence fee as a 'tax' will prove problematic for the BBC as it seeks to ensure that this generation, who will become wage-earners in the coming years, continue to contribute to the corporation's finances. They all expressed their willingness to pay for the content they like and professed to eschew piracy.

The group was clear as to how it saw the BBC. "What I hate most, is that it's old-fashioned, mumsy and patronising," admitted one contributor. "Yes, it's fuddy-duddy," agreed another. One source of annoyance was programme interstitials, with the suggestion that this was just 'propaganda'. "I have no patience for it."

Indicating perhaps that there is a misconception as to the BBC's status, one participant ventured that "the BBC is run by the government and I don't trust the Government, so I definitely don't trust the BBC. They are not independent and they spew out propaganda," with another saying: "They certainly don't represent people like us".

Another felt the BBC was "too political". "We don't feel we're getting the whole story from the BBC; it only panders to small section and everyone else feels disenfranchised," was one observation.

"It's non-inclusive, it's left-wing, London-centric and not an organisation for young people," was one accusation. "They are like the Civil Service," suggested one. "Their content is rubbish; they make it for themselves, not for us," ventured another, who added: "They need to function like a business, and sell us what we want".

For some participants, it was not necessarily the BBC's content that was the problem, but the platform itself. "I'll watch BBC content on Netflix, because it is legal," admitted one. The multiplicity of SVOD options is also problematic. "All these different platforms are a pain; we just want one or two for everything," complained one.

Back in November 2018, Sharon White, then Ofcom CEO, called for UK public service broadcasters (PSBs) to form a combined catch-up platform in order to be more like Netflix. On-demand provider BritBox was launched in the UK in 2019 but the PSBs still have their own catch-up platforms. And since then Disney+ has joined Netflix and Prime Video in the SVOD marketplace, further complicating the ease of access issue.

In describing what content this sample consumes - and how - Netflix, Amazon, YouTube, Tik Tok and Starz were mentioned as popular platforms, and apps. "I like to binge a series, not waste a whole week," admitted one. "There's a lot of [BBC] content that's not relevant. YouTube gives each person what they want to see and there's far more of it."

Of those who were familiar with the UK PSB online services, ITV Hub was not favoured. "There are too many ads, it's hard to navigate and there is too much junk," was a typical gripe, which suggests that any form of ad-supported BBC platform is not in favour. The group was not impressed by ads overall, with a number admitting to using ad-blockers.

Suggesting that the BBC operates a 'long-tail' model, one contributor said that the BBC tends "only to go where there's a big audience", with the group agreeing that they want "very niche content".

Although there is an indication that this generation is willing to pay for BBC content, a hybrid, AVOD (advertisement based video on demand) would not appear to be an option. Those favouring YouTube found people on the platform "very knowledgeable", saying that you can engage and talk with the people who made the video and they will talk back. Authenticity and engagement were important, with users often going to the 'Comments' section first to discover their peers' thoughts.

In terms of sharing views on content, it is worth noting that the discussion took place just before the BBC launched its BBC Together initiative, designed to enable family, friends, and classmates to watch and listen to BBC programmes together even when they are apart, enabling people to watch and listen to video and audio content from iPlayer, Sounds, Bitesize, news and sport at exactly the same time.

A later follow-up with a smaller section of the group ascertained that, novel though the idea was, it didn't really chime with their viewing habits and social interactions. "We go to Tik Tok and YouTube because we can say what we think. It's not curated. The BBC is like it's run by teachers; Tik Tok and YouTube are more like the playground. You can chat with your friends, it's real, it's now, it's relevant," was the verdict. "No-one I know watches the BBC, it's not what we talk about. We talk about what's on Netflix," one revealed. "When Netflix releases a big show, we're all talking about it and Instagramming," another added.

And the future?

The idea of communal, shared viewing was a somewhat alien concept, with few admitting to watching linear TV with friends and family. "I watch on my own although sometimes I do watch movies with others," was the closest admission. As to availability and relevance of content, the market-leading SVODs were favoured. "There's loads to watch on Amazon and Netflix. The recommendations on [those platforms] work really well," was one testimonial.

Although expressing a willingness to pay for content, the omens do not look good for BritBox. "Why should they charge for things made years ago?" It is apparent that this group don't watch content with other people, they watch it on their own, but they want to share it and talk about it afterwards. The idea of sitting down and watching something on TVs went out about ten years ago; they are watching on mobile devices. "They have no future in their current form," contended one. "It's not too late for them to change, but they need to do things they are not willing to do. They are too blinkered and too deaf."

Summarising the discussion, it was clear that the group had no confidence that the BBC understands their generation or was willing to change; and even if it were willing to change, that would not be enough to make them want to pay the licence fee.

What emerged was that if the BBC called it a subscription, and said it would cost £12 a month to subscribe to this content service, the group would see it completely differently. It was a choice to subscribe, not an enforced action.

There is a misunderstanding that their generation is pirating; they don't need to do that

THE GENERATION GAME

anymore. There is so much content available that they can view legally. This generation are also content creators. Platforms such as YouTube, Tik Tok and Instagram take up a lot of their time. They are interacting and creating content of their own. Initiatives such as BBC Together may go some way to re-engaging this generation, but the problem of content relevance still remains an issue.

In closing, one parent and offspring who contributed to the discussion agreed with the earlier observation regarding Peter Capaldi replacing Matt Smith as Doctor Who, led to their break from linear TV, suggesting the move typified the decreasing relevance of the BBC. A regeneration too far perhaps? The corporation's 'Doctors' have regenerated; the question now is: "Can the BBC?"

About the writer

Colin Mann has more than 40 years' experience in the media and communications industries. His early career was with BT in a range of commercial and regulatory roles, in particular with the cable and satellite TV unit, long before the telco became a broadcaster in its own right.

Operating as an independent consultant since 1990, his clients have included satellite TV channels, telcos and cable TV operators. He has edited Euromedia magazine since 2000 and is an associate editor of advanced-television. com. He also acts as media analyst for specialist consultancy Omnisperience.

Colin is a Fellow of the Society of Broadband Professionals (SCTE) and a member of both the Royal Television Society and Broadcasting Press Guild.

He can be contacted on

colinmann@cix co.uk;

Twittter@colincmann

THE SESAME STREET EFFECT.

What it means for UK broadcasters and their black and Asian audiences

MARCUS RYDER
—

UK broadcasters are losing their BAME (Black, Asian and Minority Ethnic) audiences because they are valuing individual characters and actors instead of championing rich diverse communities – a lesson one of the most influential of children's programmes learnt 50 years ago. Marcus Ryder explains:

There is no doubt that British broadcasting is some of the best in the world. I love a lot of the programmes the BBC, ITV, Channel 4 and Channel 5 produce. But the truth is, as a black person, on an emotional level, the BBC and the other broadcasters lost me the year before I was even born.

The year was 1970. That year Sesame Street launched, with an opening scene of a black male teacher in a suit, walking a young black girl, Sally, down the street and introducing her to a multicultural neighbourhood. They walk to his home and he introduces her to his black wife, who gives Sally cookies and milk.

From the very first frame, *Sesame Street* put an aspirational, professional black couple at the heart of its programme. And by doing so, it captured my heart.

In contrast, during the 1970s, on a Saturday morning I would flick between *Multi-Coloured Swap Shop* and *Tiswas* but neither had my undying loyalty. I was neither a *Blue Peter* nor even a *Magpie* child, the two flagship children's programmes of BBC or ITV respectively.

Despite being born and raised in London I looked across the Atlantic and saw myself reflected back at me and in a reality I wanted to be part of. I looked at programmes filmed just down the road from where I lived and failed to find an emotional connection.

I had no conscious understanding of race but something in Sesame Street resonated with me. It got something right in 1970 which British television still fails to grasp.

Over the last 50 years there has been real progress, with most British drama writers now recognising that there should be positive black characters. Casting directors are now more willing to cast black actors in non-stereotypical positive roles. Things are far from perfect, but there is no denying that progression. We see positive black characters on our screen relatively often – from actors in *Dr Who* to *The Hustle* and of course Luther. However, there's something special about these positive characters.

How communities are portrayed

They are often the only black character, inhabiting functioning white communities, or at the very least majority white communities. Black communities on TV on the other hand are portrayed almost exclusively as dysfunctional. While many of the people portrayed in a drama set in a BAME community may be likable, the community they were set in is normally anything but.

The message that comes across loud and clear on our screens is that while there might be good black individuals, black communities are a problem. It suggests that if you are a good or positive black person you should want to leave the dysfunctional black communities as quickly as possible.

While some might downplay these unspoken messages, the reality is one comes across these implicit negative views about black communities all the time. There are often similar messages about South Asians on TV, while there might be positive individuals from the Indian sub-continent, the communities are invariably problematic, populated with forced marriages and potential terrorists. And unfortunately, in the UK, East Asian representation is still so thin on the ground it is almost impossible to discuss it sensibly.

Yet the reality is that while dysfunctional black communities certainly do exist, there are also incredibly good positive functional communities. Analysis by Dr Nicola Rollock into the black middle class offers strong examples of functional positive black communities that rarely see our TV screens. I for one am very proud to be part of a black community that includes lawyers, film makers, policemen, civil servants, charity workers – but also unemployed people. It's mixed, but positively so.

British public service broadcasters (PSBs) are on the edge of a precipice. In 2018 the media regulator Ofcom warned that they were at risk of losing a generation of viewers, as younger audiences under 30 turned away from the traditional broadcasters and opted to watch Netflix, Amazon and other SVODs (subscription video on demand) instead, as well as other online content.

Also, according to another recent report by the UK media regulator, when it comes to diversity British audiences are increasingly finding better representation and authentic portrayal on Netflix and other online video-streaming providers. Every executive I speak to at a PSB is aware of these statistics and recognises the need to address them.

However, in my experience they do not fully grasp the problem facing them with regards to BAME viewers. They know the BAME viewing figures are worse than their white equivalents but they normally just attribute this to the fact that the BAME community is proportionately younger than the overall white UK population and just see it as part of the wider problem of losing their younger audience.

However, I believe the problem is far deeper than this.

In the 1970s I might not have been in love with the BBC or ITV and I might have wished I lived on Sesame Street but, with only three terrestrial channels, I was stuck in the UK. There was no way I could move to the functional, beautiful, multicultural neighbourhood populated with black teachers and children that looked just like me.

But now, in 2020, our younger children can move to Sesame Street whenever they want. And our older children can see aspirational black communities on HBO's Insecure or ABC's *Black-ish*. So why aren't these positive, broader messages about our diverse communities coming out on UK PSBs?

Black-ish

What Netflix is getting right

Why have online providers been able to learn from the lessons of Sesame Street and build upon them while legacy broadcasters like the BBC, ITV and Channel 4, still seem to be failing their ethnically diverse audiences?

Are the executives and commissioners at the SVODs and online providers more enlightened and receptive to diversity compared to their counterparts at the BBC, ITV, Channel 4 and Channel 5?

While people are important, I very much doubt that the difference can be attributed to just the different attitudes of a few individuals and commissioners. For one thing many of the commissioners and senior gatekeepers at the SVODs are from the PSBs originally and flip back and forth between the different types of broadcasters.

Instead, I believe the answer can be found in the different economic models between traditional broadcasters versus online video streamers.

Amanda Lotz, a professor of media studies at the University of Michigan, analysed Netflix's economic model in 2017 and argued that traditional broadcasters still think in terms of attracting large audiences for a single programme as advertisers pay for eyeballs. As an American she didn't look at the BBC but I would argue the same argument applies as the BBC still looks to large audiences to justify its licence fee.

Online streamers like Netflix and Amazon – on the other hand – are not pursuing large audiences for advertisers. Instead, they are trying to maximize subscribers.

Quoted in The Conversation, Professor Lotz says: "To succeed, subscriber-funded services must offer enough programming that viewers find the service worthy of their monthly fee. Each show doesn't need a mass audience – which is the measure of success for advertiser-funded television – but the service does need to provide enough value that subscribers continue to pay."

Professor Lotz describes the strategy Netflix employs as 'conglomerated niche' and says that because it does not broadcast in a linear fashion most subscribers don't even know most of Netflix's content and only concentrate on the series that appeal to them.

She uses the metaphor of a library to describe this phenomenon: "If you were to ask different Netflix subscribers about the service's brand, you'd likely get different responses. There is no one Netflix; rather, think of it as an expansive library with many small nooks and rooms. Most subscribers never wander floor to floor. Instead, they stay in the corner that matches their tastes."

THE GENERATION GAME

The strength of niche audiences

This means channel executives at traditional broadcasters think completely differently when it comes to commissioning content versus commissioners at Netflix. The BBC executive, for example, is thinking: "Will the programme get a large audience?" while the Netflix executive is thinking: "Will this new series be able to get a new different section of the audience to subscribe?"

The Netflix execs are constantly seeking out programmes that will get a different niche audience to subscribe or continue to subscribe.

Take my favourite series at the moment Insecure, which I mentioned earlier. It finally tipped the balance for me to finally take out a subscription for HBO Go and I am sure I am not the only one. *Insecure* is therefore a win for HBO, in a way that commissioning yet another 'non-diverse' programme would not be, as it wouldn't attract new subscribers.

Compare this to ITV or BBC. All things being equal the ITV and BBC commissioners would prefer to commission another series like Call the Midwife as it would bring in a far larger audience, even if it is the same old non-diverse audience that already watches the majority of their programmes, than commission Insecure, which relatively speaking would be a ratings flop.

Television executives could even make *Call the Midwife* more ethnically diverse by adding a few Caribbean nurses. This is the type of diversity that is often favoured by executives as it broadens the programme's appeal without risking the core audience. However, this approach does not address the fundamental Sesame Street strategy of creating a community.

For this reason, the SVODs approach leads to far deeper diverse programmes being commissioned by broadcasters who are financed by subscribers. The irony is that in targeting niche audiences streaming services often create quality content, which over time has a far wider appeal.

If you talk to executives of traditional broadcasters, they all recognise the importance of commissioning for non-linear viewing and targeting certain demographics. But it is still incredibly hard for commissioners to break out of a linear 'big-audiences-matter' state of mind.

The truth is as traditional broadcasters worry about big audiences now, they risk having no audiences in the future. Only by recognizing the rich diversity of their audiences, and creating programmes that they want to watch, will broadcasters survive. Sesame Street may have been launched in a time before SVODs but its entire model has been based around this idea.

Just two years after Sesame Street began in America it launched a Brazilian version. Importantly, it did not simply dub the American version into Portuguese or add a few Brazilian characters. It relocated into a new community that reflected Brazil's diversity.

It has repeated the same trick in at least 34 different countries including South Africa, Russia, Palestine and Israel. Interestingly, the UK broadcasters consistently rejected working with the producers of Sesame Street and so there was never a British version I could identify with. Instead I fell in love with the American one.

I will leave you with one more Sesame Street-related fact.

When the first episode of Sesame Street was

aired in 1970 the US was 87.65 per cent white. According to the last census conducted in 2010 it is now 72.40 per cent white.

The year I was born, 1971, was the first time the UK census specifically gathered ethnicity data. That year they found the white population made up roughly 97.7 per cent of the population. Today the BAME population in the UK is 13 per cent, a larger percentage than the non-white US population at the time Sally first met all the Sesame Street characters in the first episode.

In 1970 a children's television show had already worked out the importance of appealing to the country's non-white population, an appeal that made a small child born in London a year later fall in love with it.

British broadcasters do not have the luxury of waiting another 50 years to finally work out what Sesame Street got right. Because unlike 50 years ago Sesame Street is literally just one channel hop away, as is all the other great diverse content that prioritises community representation over simple diverse representation of individuals.

About the writer

Marcus Ryder is an award-winning executive producer at Caixin Global, China's leading financial publication. He is a visiting professor in media diversity at Birmingham City University and was a core member of the executive committee to launch the Sir Lenny Henry Centre for Media Diversity.

He has worked in television for more than 25 years. For eight years he oversaw BBC Scotland's current affairs documentaries where he formulated his ideas on the importance of diverse representation championing communities as opposed to simply increasing the representation of different types of individuals.

THE GENERATION GAME

THE EDITORS

Michael Wilson

Michael Wilson is an experienced chief executive, managing director, board member and editor-in-chief with more than 30 years' business and leadership experience in the content creation, broadcasting, media, communications and digital sectors. He has held senior roles at national and international level including Sky News, Five News, UTV Northern Ireland and ITV.

He now runs a consultancy business specialising in content and platform strategy specifically working with the boards and C-levels leaders of major international businesses. He is also the CEO of the Isle of Media, the national development agency for the Isle of Man digital and creative industries. For more than a decade he was managing director of the ITV region in Northern Ireland – UTV - and represented UTV on the board of ITV Network. He is Managing Director of fine art business Paul Yates Art, and an Entrepreneur in Residence at Catalyst, the Northern Ireland Science Park.

He sits on the Royal Television Society's Centre's council and is a founder member of the Irish Film and Television Academy. His programming has won Baftas, RTS's awards and New York Television Festival Awards. He's a published contributing author, media and business commentator and currently lives in Switzerland.

Neil Fowler

Neil Fowler has been in journalism since graduation, starting life as trainee reporter on the Leicester Mercury. He went on to edit four regional dailies, including The Journal in the north east of England and The Western Mail in Wales. He was then publisher of The Toronto Sun in Canada before returning to the UK to edit Which? magazine.

In 2010/11 he was the Guardian Research Fellow at Oxford University's Nuffield College where he investigated the decline and future of regional and local newspapers in the UK. From then until 2016 he helped organise the college's prestigious David Butler media and politics seminars. As well as being an occasional contributor to trade magazines he now acts as an adviser to organisations on their management and their external and internal communications and media policies and strategies.

AFTERLIFE

There are some who leave their marks in the hearts and lives of the audience, who become iconic or for whom children's media is important. We pay tribute to a few whose contribution was immeasurable, and who sadly passed away in 2020.

Renee Fisher on Unsplash

AFTERLIFE

Michael Angelis

REMEMBERING MICHAEL ANGELIS
April 29th 1944 – May 30th 2020

SHARON MILLER

When I heard Michael Angelis had died, on May 30th this year, I stopped and remembered, with great sadness and affection, the days I had been privileged to spend with Michael when I was Head Writer and Voice Director on *Thomas and Friends*.

Michael was an actor of extraordinary talent but it was as the voice of the Storyteller in Thomas the Tank Engine, the iconic Children's television series, that he became known and loved the world over.

For twenty-one years, from 1991 to 2012, Michael's Storyteller was the heartbeat and signature of Thomas. His voice signalled to parents that their children would be safe and entranced in his company, for ten minutes of storytelling bliss.

These were the days – and they were many – when Thomas was live action, not animated. The engines' faces didn't move: only their eyes gave expression, as they swivelled from side to side, up and down.

So, the 'animation' was Michael's voice. It gave the engine's their characters, revealed their inner thoughts and outer actions and charted the adventure of each story. His voice was different for each engine – and, of course, for The Fat Controller. But the vocal shift was subtle and came from an understanding of each character, not reliant on vocal gimmick. You knew instantly which engine was speaking. And most remarkably of all, Michael's voice told the audience that he cared about the engines – and liked them. His voice was the cornerstone of the series.

Michael was extremely modest about his role on Thomas. Never more so than with the widespread, and still held, assumption that the voice of the Storyteller was Ringo Starr. He'd shake his head and smile. "I know. Well…we're all just Scousers, you see…"

Michael Angelis was so much more than that. He was – and will always be - the voice of so many childhoods.

AFTERLIFE

Derek Fowlds

DEREK FOWLDS
2 September 1937 - 17 January 2020

DIANA HINSHELWOOD

Derek Fowlds, the first side-kick of the much-loved Basil Brush, passed away earlier this year at the age of 82. He was best known as a serious actor in shows such as *Yes Minister* and *Heart Beat*, but it is as "Mr Derek", the straight man to Basil Brush's mischievous fox puppet in *The Basil Brush Show* that Derek is best known to a certain generation.

Basil made a surprise appearance at Derek's funeral to pay tribute to his friend and read a poem remembering the good times they had making the show. Of course, Basil introduced humour into his eulogy, saying "Stars begged to be in our show, that much is not contested. Big names of the 70s, even some who weren't arrested."

Fowlds had spoken fondly of his time on the show and in an interview in 2000 called the puppet his best mate. He told actor's bible *The Stage*: "People think that I must somehow resent Basil Brush, but I don't, not at all. I'd go as far to say that for four years he was my best mate and all I've ever done is wish him well."

For four years (1969-73) Derek stoically put up with Basil's bad jokes and puns, followed with his catchphrase: "Boom! Boom!" He was a perfect foil for Basil's humour, and the pair became household names in a children's show that was rare for the time in the unpatronising way it treated its audience. It was often irreverent and not afraid to use political humour. Mr Derek and Basil Brush will pass into Children's TV History as an iconic duo.

I'll leave the last word to Basil, with a quote from his poem dedicated to Mr Derek.

> "I'll interrupt no more, Old Chum, the stage is now all yours.
>
> That sound we love, it's all for you, for Mr Derek, applause."

AFTERLIFE

LORD GORDON OF STRATHBLANE
Farewell to a Friend

APPG ORGANISER JAYNE KIRKHAM PAYS TRIBUTE TO A SUPPORTER OF CHILDREN'S MEDIA AND THE ARTS

It is with great sadness that we learned of the death of Lord Gordon of Strathblane after contracting coronavirus. He was a long standing supporter of the All Party Parliamentary Group for Children's Media and the Arts and was someone the Group could rely on to uphold its principles.

The APPG co-chairs pay tribute:

"Lord Gordon was a passionate advocate for children's media and the creative industries, and he always always spoke intelligently, with conviction and with kindness.

He will be remembered extremely fondly by colleagues, friends and everyone who came into contact with him. He will be truly missed."

Julie Elliott MP, Member of Parliament for Sunderland Central

"Lord Gordon and I were members of the House of Lords Select Communication Committee for several years. During that time, he always gave strong support for issues concerning children's media and those working in this important part of the creativity industry.

"He was a man of wisdom, vision and spoke with common sense and compassion. He leaves a lasting legacy throughout the industry and his drive and passion will be truly missed."

Baroness Floella Benjamin, DBE

CHILDREN'S MEDIA YEARBOOK 202-

YOU DID IT!
CONTRIBUTORS

YOU DID IT!

Bruna Capozzoli

Bruna Capozzoli heads up CAKE's digital division, Popcorn Digital. As Creative Director, she provides creative solutions for kids' entertainment brands establishing and expanding their pres-ence in the digital space.

Applying her solid experience in content creation and audience development as well as a di-verse background in film-making and theatre, Bruna works with leading kids' brands designing tailored strategies to produce original, challenging and engaging online content.

Prior to joining Popcorn Digital, Bruna worked with leading digital producer Diagonal View and global phenomenon 'Talking Tom and Friends' at Outfit7.

Greg Childs

Greg Childs worked for over 25 years at the BBC, mainly as a director, producer and executive producer of children's programmes. He created the first children's BBC websites and, as Head of Children's Digital, developed and launched the children's channels CBBC and CBeebies.

Greg left the BBC in 2004 and subsequently advised producers on digital, interactive, and cross-platform strategies; and broadcasters on channel launches, digital futures and management support.

He was in the launch team for Teachers TV and the CITV Channel in the UK, and was advisor to the Al Jazeera Children's Channel for three years consulting with the European Broadcasting Union on their Children's and Youth strategy.

Greg has been Editorial Director of the Children's Media Conference for the last fifteen years. He is also one the Heads of Studies at the German Akademie Fur Kindermedien and is Director of the audience advocacy body – the Children's Media Foundation.
.

Cressida Cowell

Cressida Cowell is the author-illustrator of the 'How to Train Your Dragon' and 'The Wizards of Once' book series. 'How to Train Your Dragon' is also an Academy Award nominated film and TV franchise. Cressida is a trustee of World Book Day, a patron of Read for Good, and an ambassador for the National Literacy Trust and the Woodland Trust. She has won the Ruth Rendell Award for championing literacy, the Blue Peter Book Award, and the Hay Festival Medal for Fiction. She is an honorary fellow of Keble College, Oxford, and has an honorary doctorate from the University of Brighton. Cressida is the current Waterstones Children's Laureate (2019-2022).

Zoë Daniel

Zoë is a 21 year old writer and freelance multimedia journalist with bylines in The Guardian and Reuters. She was named "an Inspirational Teen you should follow on Instagram" by the London Evening Standard following a social media campaign she worked on with Instagram UK. Zoë runs online magazine www.zoezine.com which in the future hopes to use as a tool to amplify the voices of creatives from marginalised backgrounds.

Zoë works and travels with the EU Intellectual Property Office's Ideas Powered Initiative and recently contributed to The Digital Fairy's trend report into Gen Z.

Kate Dimbleby

Kate co-founded Stornaway Productions with Rupert Howe after many years of frustration with how hard it is to make interactive films. In May 2020, they launched Stornaway, a scripting and production tool to enable producers to create and deliver interactive films easily and affordably with no coding.

Stornaway are currently working with producers and broadcasters to develop interactive films for SVODs in all genres.

Kate has worked as a producer, writer and performer for over two decades. She has recorded six albums, and has toured the world with theatrical music shows, working with world-class musicians, writers and other artists to tell stories about women's voices. Kate has also developed a structure for writing and developing her ideas to allow for maximum creative freedom and flexibility particularly live on stage. This is at the heart of Stornaway's interactive writing tools, particularly how they've developed the Story Map and Story Islands™.

Jackie Edwards

Jackie is Head of the BFI Young Audiences Content Fund, and is responsible for the successful implementation of this game changing UK Government initiative to stimulate the provision of public service content for audiences of 0-18,
Jackie joined the BFI from BBC Children's where she had been the Head of Acquisitions and Independent Animation, responsible for pre-buying and acquiring live-action and animated programming for CBeebies, CBBC and iPlayer. She joined the BBC in 2008 as Content Manager and Executive Producer. Prior to the BBC Jackie was a producer in the Independent Sector. A passionate advocate for public service content, Jackie is living her dream job!

Lucy Edwards

Lucy Edwards is a presenter, YouTuber and disability rights campaigner who is usually accompanied by her guide dog named Olga. After losing her eyesight, Lucy started her own YouTube channel to document her life. She now has 35,000 subscribers and over 3 million views of her videos. In December 2019, Lucy became the first blind presenter on BBC Radio 1. Her other credits include 'In Touch' (BBC Radio 4), 'Click' (BBC World News) and 'The Travel Show' (BBC World News). She also works as a freelance producer for the BBC. Lucy was the first blind ambassador for CoverGirl and has written for The Sunday Times as well as publishing the first ever 'Blind Beauty Guide' book. Lucy has supported charities such as Guide Dogs UK, Vision Foundation and RNIB. Lucy is passionate about promoting disability issues having overcome her own adversity to show the world that there is life after sight loss.
Lucy's call to action:
Lucyedwardsoffficial.com/disabilitychangemakers

Helen Foulkes

Helen Foulkes is Head of BBC Education overseeing BBC Bitesize, BBC Teach, BBC Food and the BBC's educational campaigns. Our aim is to 'Transform lives through Education'. BBC Bitesize is the most used educational website in the UK, which is used by 80% of secondary school students; BBC Teach supports teachers with world class, curriculum linked content for use in the classroom; and education campaigns that address a societal or educational deficit, from Ten Pieces and Super Movers to BBC micro:bit.
Prior to working in BBC Education Helen has a wide range of Television Executive Producer credits including Points of View, Country Tracks, See Hear and To Buy or Not to Buy. Before becoming an executive she worked across a multitude of BBC brands such as Holiday, Homefront and What Not to Wear.

Maxine Fox

As Managing Director of Giraffe Insights, an international research agency, specialising in youth, kids and family insight, Maxine leads a dedicated team working across a number of disciplines. With over a decade working in research, she has become an industry recognised specialist in speaking to kids, young people and families to elicit the greatest insights for brands.

Nathan Guy

As Managing Director of Giraffe Nathan Guy has been working as a drama teacher and creative specialist in primary schools full time for 7 years with over 15 years' experience of teaching, coaching and mentoring young people through various different theatre groups and organisations. After graduating from Royal Central School of Speech and Drama, Nathan mainly tried to focus his acting efforts on playing fun, cheeky, characters and aiming to become unexpected heroes: to possess ultimate strength; to obtain a magical flying red capes; to track down and rescue missing animals; to

YOU DID IT!

be the top cat who can be heard on the roof but in fact to be all the while curled up by the fire ...

He is driven specifically to encourage new, young, diverse and disengaged audiences' participation in the arts locally, nationally and globally.

He was born and raised in east London and is a big fan of broccoli, fish and chips and Tik Tok.

Diana Hinshelwood

Diana has worked in Children's Media for over 30 years on well-known Children's programmes such as "Record Breakers" "Grange Hill" "Going Live" and "Playdays". She joined CBeebies as an On-Air producer at the launch of the channel in 2002, and in 2006 collaborated with Children's Radio to create and launch CBeebies Radio. On leaving the BBC, Diana worked on "Lazytown", "Sarah and Duck" and "The Fluffy Club" and developed TV and Radio projects. She also produced for digital platforms such as Espresso Education (Now Discovery) and Open University, and is currently a freelance development producer and scriptwriter, winning 2 commissions from CBeebies Radio and option agreements for animations. Diana is the Newsletter Editor of the Children's Media Foundation Newsletter, and a member of the CMF Executive Group.

Anna Home OBE

Anna began working for the BBC in 1960 and started working in the children's department in 1964. She has won many accolades, including a BAFTA Lifetime Achievement award. Anna was the first Chair of the BAFTA Children's Committee, and has chaired both the EBU Chil-dren's and Youth Working Group and the Prix Jeunesse International Advisory Board. She was also the Chair of the Save The Kids' TV Campaign Executive Committee and the Showcomotion chil-dren's media conference.

She now chairs the Board of the Children's Media Conference and the Children's Media Founda-tion, and is a Board member of Screen South.

Chris Jarvis

Chris Jarvis has haunted Children's TV for over 26 years starting in 'The Broom Cupboard' then 'Look Sharp', 'Wood Lane', 'Playdays', 'The Friday Zone', 'Fully Booked', 'Jungle Run', 'Dream Street' and 'Maths Mansion'. In 2002 he joined CBeebies to host 'Step Inside' and, most recently, 'Show Me Show Me', 'CBeebies Stargazing' and another 'CBeebies Prom' later this month. Behind the scenes Chris writes pantomimes and TV shows including the award winning 'Old Jack's Boat' inspired by a song written by his dad.

Hazel Kenyon

Hazel Kenyon is Director of the UK and Ireland Book Research business. She started at Nielsen Book in 2009 as a Publisher Account Manager working with a portfolio of clients to help them analyse the BookScan sales data. She is now responsible for all UK and Ireland client relationships in publishing, retail and media and for strategic business development across all the research products measuring changes in print, digital and consumer behaviour. Hazel started her career as a Space Physicist, working in industry and academia and for her PhD analysed particle data from the Cassini spacecraft during its grand tour of Saturn.

Jayne Kirkham

With over thirty years' experience working with and writing for children and young people, Jayne's commissions have ranged in size from small conservation films in Africa to international feature films with TV credits including 'Bing' and 'Treasure Champs'. The past year has been spent writing for Showtown – Blackpool's new museum of Fun and Entertainment, opening in 2021. She is a member of the CMF Board and in 2011 established the All Party Parliamentary Group for Children's Media and the Arts.

CHILDREN'S MEDIA YEARBOOK 202-

David Kleeman

Strategist, analyst, author, speaker, once and future traveler, connector — David Kleeman has led the children's media industry in developing sustainable, child-friendly practices for 35+ years. As SVP of Global Trends for strategy/research consultancy and digital studio Dubit, David is passionate about kids' evolving possibilities for entertainment, engagement, play and learning, while recognising that child development remains constant.

David is advisory board chair to the international children's TV festival PRIX JEUNESSE and on Boards of the 2021 World Summit on Media for Children, the National Association for Media Literacy Education and the Children's Media Association.

Ryan Lewis

Ryan monitors performance and aids development of the BBC's bespoke content for children as well as being an audience expert on the children's audiences for the rest of the business. He joined in 2011, working with Sport across the London 2012 Olympics and on the relaunching of BBC ID and profiles. His time in Children's includes supporting the launch of CBeebies Playtime, the BBC's biggest investment in children's for a generation and the recent redesign of iPlayer profiles for children.

Helen Lockett

Helen is Research Manager at Discovery, and a core member of The Hub, Discovery's kids and youth offering. She is passionate about youth research, with experience covering a broad range of sectors including media, finance, education and more. Helen combines her extensive quantitative experience with qualitative insights, to deep dive into what kids are doing and why. She uses a variety of research techniques to gain practical insights, helping brands to understand young people and how to engage with them.

Pete Maginin

Pete has extensive kids, youth and insight experience, having worked in and headed up insight teams agency side for 18 years at Illuminas and The Pineapple Lounge. He has worked with kids, teens and family focussed brands in the UK and globally for clients including Sky, Netflix, Disney Channel, BBC, Twitch, Mattel Creations and eOne.

Pete Maginn is Director of Insight at Beano Brain, the insights consultancy from Beano Studios, using his expertise to devise the most appropriate, bespoke approaches to deliver against client briefs. He ensures that their business decisions are grounded in the most authentic insights and true understanding of their audienc-es, that in turn drives optimal engagement from kids and teens with their brands

Sharon Miller

Sharon has worked extensively as a drama television director and writer, both in Britain and Los Angeles. She now focuses on her work as a writer, voice director and casting director for lead-ing pre-school UK and International animation. Her credits include 'Thomas and Friends', 'Lily's Driftwood Bay', 'Zack and Quack', 'Fox and Hare' (Movie and Series, Netherlands), 'Numtums', 'Treasure Champs', 'Tickety Toc', 'Wissper', 'Lillybuds', 'Bob the Builder', 'Spot Bots', 'Ricky' (French/Russian) and most recently – 'Paddington' for Heyday, Studio Canal and Nickelodeon.

Ash Perrin

Ash is the founder and CEO of The Flying Seagull Project, a UK-based charity that works around the world to bring happiness to children who are underprivileged, marginalised or suffering.

They use music, arts, dance and clowning to spread smiles to more than 130,000 children in hospitals, orphanages and refugee camps around the world. Their method reflects powerful evidence from social science, neuroscience and biochemistry, witnessing first-hand the incredible transformations brought about by the power of play.

YOU DID IT!

Jessica Rees

Jessica has worked in the Market Research team at Ofcom for over six years and has experience running both quantitative and qualitative research projects. She is part of Ofcom's media litera-cy research team and leads on Ofcom's children's media literacy research which includes over-seeing Ofcom's longitudinal tracking survey into children's media literacy and ethnographic, small-scale qualitative research among children. Jessica is passionate about sharing Ofcom's re-search and supporting the work of government, organisations and agencies through research. Jessica joined Ofcom in 2012 as part of the graduate scheme and has a BSc in Psychology from the University of Liverpool.

Colin Ward

Colin is Deputy Director of the Children's Media Foundation and is responsible for the CMF's Executive Group and links with the research community. His long career in children's TV started at Yorkshire Television, working across factual, entertainment and drama formats. He won a Bafta for 'The Scoop' before joining Granada Kids to produce the Bafta-nominated gameshow 'Jungle Run'. Moving to the BBC, he won a second Bafta for the gameshow 'Raven', going on to work as an Executive Producer with CBBC Scotland on a range of entertainment and drama formats. He now combines freelance writing and directing with work as a lecturer in film and television production at the University of York. audience and experience design.

Cecilia Weiss

Cecilia has over 20 years' experience in children's television and digital educational media. She worked in BBC Schools TV as PA, director, research, and then became a producer for CBeebies Interactive. After leaving the BBC, she worked on a range of freelance projects, and is currently the editor of iChild., a website providing resources for children.

Camilla Umar

Cam is your Children's Media Yearbook 2020 designer. She divides her days between artworking and teaching movement classes. As a designer she regularly works with Sheffield Theatres, Lawrence Bately Theatre and Leeds Playhouse. The rest of the time she can be found pulling shapes in her movement studio and generally having fun.
www.cutoutandkeep.co.uk
www.movewithcam.co.uk

We need your support:
www.thechildrensmediafoundation.org

www.ingramcontent.com/pod-product-compliance
Lightning Source LLC
Chambersburg PA
CBHW040225040426
42333CB00052B/3366